"Karine Rashkovsky's *An Improbable Life: My Father's Escape from Soviet Russia* tells an important story, all the more important today as freedoms previously taken for granted seem fragile, and there is a price to be paid for being a Jew. Karine narrates her father Reuven's life in his voice, first as a talented and ambitious Jew yearning for freedom in the oppressive world of the Soviet Union, and then as a Jewish activist, seeking freedom for himself and his fellow Jews and being oppressed for that very yearning. She tells of his journey to freedom and his new life in Israel, France, and finally in Canada, The story is told with charm and depth and includes her mother's equally improbable journey and the struggles of her grandparents. It reminds us of the great achievement of the last generation, the exodus to freedom of Soviet Jews, the courage of a generation asking for the most basic of rights, the freedom to live as a Jew openly, joyfully. It reminded me of the courage it takes to confront Pharaoh, part the Sea, walk through the desert and reach the promised land."

— Dr. Michael Berenbaum, Distinguished Professor,
American Jewish University

"*An Improbable Life* is powerful, inspiring, and timely. This important contribution to Soviet, Canadian, and Jewish history and human rights is thought-provoking and jam-packed with lessons and legacies that are relevant locally and globally today. In skillfully telling Reuven's remarkable story, Rashkovsky writes from the heart, bringing to life his indomitable courage, determination, strength, and hope despite the widespread social injustices and rampant antisemitism he and his family experienced. From discrimination at school and university, to being conscripted into the Red Army, to working on fighter jets, to succeeding in fleeing Soviet Russia against all odds, to immigrating and settling in Canada and beyond, Reuven's adventurous life, survival, and success were certainly improbable. His story is a page turner, and his achievements are a poignant reminder and call to action to never give up on our dreams in the pursuit of freedom and social justice for all."

— Dr. Karlee Sapoznik Evans, Historian and
Human Rights Scholar

"Beautifully written, this is a rare first-person account of Reuven Rashkovsky, a person who managed to beat the odds by living a remarkable, successful and brave life in the circumstances which made it almost impossible. As a Jewish person born in the postwar Stalin's Soviet Union, he managed to get an education, build a family, and successfully fight to escape the country. Filled with details of everyday interactions, difficult decisions and genuine love for one's family, the book is impossible to put down. Highly recommended."

— ˙na Shternshis, Professor, University of Toronto

"A revealing, fascinating, and candid story of liberation from the burden of bureaucratically assigned Jewishness. The book is a good read for anyone, and a good source for historians of Soviet Jewry."

— Dr. Gennady Estraikh, Professor, New York University

"Karine Rashkovsky's *An Improbable Life: My Father's Escape from Soviet Russia* is a must-read tour de force. While many books have been written on Soviet life, this one is undoubtedly unique. It offers an intimate glimpse into the mid-century life of a provincial Jewish family that in the face of daily struggles to survive and pervasive antisemitism not only perseveres, but achieves academic and professional success. Radiating with the narrator's joie de vivre, this story illustrates how dedication, friendship, love, and unrelenting persistence help one person break free from the shackles of oppression. Readers are left with optimism and hope as they follow the challenges and triumphs of Reuven's resilient story which chronicles immigrating to foreign countries, adapting to new cultures and languages, and overcoming personal tragedies, all the while devotedly working to better the world around him. Rashkovsky's captivating writing style pieces together a work that is deeply cathartic for those from a similar background, and invaluable for anyone with an interest in the Soviet Jewish experience. This evocative, informative, and timeless narrative keeps readers hooked until the very last page."

— Anna Waisman, Ph.D. (Cand.) Clinical Psychology
and Neuropsychology, Vanier Canada
Graduate Scholar, York University

"*An Improbable Life* by Karine Rashkovsky is a powerful and moving tribute from a daughter to her father, Reuven Rashkovsky, who has been a source of inspiration and a heroic figure since her childhood. Narrated in Reuven's voice, the book vividly portrays the challenges and resilience of Jewish life in the Soviet Union. Reuven's journey from a brilliant mathematician denied opportunities in Moscow to his dramatic escape and new beginnings in Israel, France, and Canada is both heartwrenching and inspiring. Despite relentless antisemitism and numerous setbacks, Reuven's unwavering perseverance, ingenuity, and humor shine through. His story is a testament to the indomitable spirit of millions of Jews who faced similar struggles. This compelling narrative not only honors Reuven's life but also serves as a poignant reminder of the enduring human quest for dignity and freedom. A must-read for anyone interested in history, perseverance, and the triumph of the human spirit."

— Alex Maizlish, Ph.D., Vanier Scholar,
Mathematics and Data Science

"Karine Rashkovsky's *An Improbable Life: My Father's Escape from Soviet Russia* is an excellent biography of Reuven Rashkovsky. Reuven was born to a Jewish family in Uzbekistan, where his parents were evacuated during the war. He grew up in the provincial city Belgorod-Dnestrovsky, Ukraine, where he often encountered anti-semitism. Rashkovsky studied at the University of Odesa, and although he was an excellent student, after graduation he was not accepted to a Ph.D. program because he was Jewish. His desire to live in a free world brought Reuven to the Soviet Jewry emigration movement. With great difficulty and risk of being arrested by the KGB, he and other activists escaped from the Soviet Union to Israel. Reuven's life had many other improbable twists and turns including his participation in the Yom Kippur War, his work in tech, and his time teaching at various educational institutions in Israel, France and Canada. This is an amazing life and journey, with many unpredictable ups and downs, and unforeseeable suffering and jubilation."

— Dr. Victoria Khiterer, Professor of History,
Millersville University

"*An Improbable Life* offers a succinct and compelling account, showcasing how threads of family, friends, mentors, social institutions, political oppression, and antisemitism formed the tapestry of Reuven Rashkovsky's life. Straightforward descriptions of living circumstances, academic, and professional pursuits amidst shifting political regimes, international wars, and spanning four continents are woven together in this engaging and informative narrative, highlighting how individual lives unfold within broader national and global contexts. Ultimately focusing on lived experiences shaped by happenstance, tragedy, hope, and effort, this book offers a glimpse into times past, invites important contemporary philosophical considerations, and serves as a profound testimony to the underlying beauty of hope and human resilience."

— Dr. Jonathan S. Marion, Professor of Anthropology,
Steps Along the Way

"The detailed color and engaging scenes Karine Rashkovsky brings to each chapter immerses readers in a powerful look into Reuven's life. The intimacy she brings to his stories, about say, being a soldier in Russia or the tense escape to Israel, invigorates the book with drama that makes these key moments in his life so compelling to read. What Karine has done with this book is not just an ode to her brave father but also give readers an in-depth cinematic view into areas of the world that dominate headlines today."

— David Silverberg, former artistic director and founder
of Toronto Poetry Project, author, and journalist

"I was thoroughly engaged by the story of Dr. Reuven Rashkovsky's improbable life, and moved by his daughter's devotion to the telling. Reuven provides a vivid picture of the disadvantages and vicissitudes, large and small, that Jews in the Soviet Union encountered on a daily basis. His description of his escape, well before large numbers of Jews were allowed to leave, is riveting. And as an educator, I was intrigued by his account of how the innovative and successful Brain Power enrichment program grew from its origin in his basement, and his mind. A highly satisfying read."

— Dr. Sandra R. Schecter, Professor Emerita,
Faculty of Education, York University

"'Jews are just like everyone else, only more so.' A catchy quote attributed to Lionel Blue, a British rabbi, journalist and broadcaster, and the first thought that came to my mind upon finishing Dr. Rashkovsky's record of her father Reuven's life. Having had the privilege of meeting Reuven in person, I've always found him interesting. Well, now I know that the meager interesting doesn't come close to describing just how extraordinary a person he is, and how tumultuous—and, indeed, improbable—his life has been. This memoir depicts in great detail—not as a detached academic study, nor as a speculative work of fiction, but through a lived, first-person experience—the dehumanizing monstrosity of the Soviet regime, especially where it came to its antisemitic nature."

— Alex Tsirulnikov, author of *The E Apocrypha* novel series

"This is an excellent and brutally honest reflection. Reuven's story is extraordinary. It highlights the experiences of thousands of talented Jews who escaped the Soviet Union and Warsaw Bloc countries. These people had an unparalleled impact on science, education, and culture in the West. I hope that this book will evoke deep reflections among Americans and Canadians on how ideologically charged culture and propaganda full of hatred and antisemitism make us, descendants of Reuven's generation, feel today."

— Dr. Ruslan Dorfman, MBA, CSO at Pillcheck, Adjunct
Professor at Department of Anesthesia, McMaster University

"This book will resonate particularly well with those who either lived through, or were involved with, the Soviet Jewry movement in the United States. I know now that the time I spent advocating for Soviet Jewry was time well spent. This book demonstrates the difference between life and opportunity in an authoritarian society and life and accomplishment in a western, liberal society.

So improbable were the events that occurred in Reuven's life that if I were watching a movie, I would have assumed that the screenwriter had taken liberty with the facts for 'dramatic effect.'

Despite initially planning to skim the book for this endorsement, after reading just a few pages, I realized how much my own life would be enhanced by reading the whole book! I did so, and I recommend that others should do so, too."

— Dr. Ira Sheskin, Professor, Department of Geography and
Sustainable Development, University of Miami

AN IMPROBABLE LIFE

MY FATHER'S ESCAPE FROM SOVIET RUSSIA

AN IMPROBABLE LIFE

MY FATHER'S ESCAPE FROM SOVIET RUSSIA

DR. KARINE RASHKOVSKY

CHERRY ORCHARD BOOKS

2024

Library of Congress Cataloging-in-Publication Data

Names: Rashkovsky, Karine, 1978- author.

Title: An improbable life : my father's escape from Soviet Russia / Karine Rashkovsky.

Other titles: My father's escape from Soviet Russia

Description: Boston: Cherry Orchard Books, 2024.

Identifiers: LCCN 2024006078 (print) | LCCN 2024006079 (ebook) | ISBN 9798887195124 (hardback) | ISBN 9798887195131 (paperback) | ISBN 9798887195148 (adobe pdf) | ISBN 9798887195155 (epub)

Subjects: LCSH: Rashkovsky, Reuven, 1945- | Jews--Soviet Union--Biography. | Mathematicians--Soviet Union--Biography. | Jews--Soviet Union--Social conditions. | Soviet Union--History--1953-1985. | Immigrants--Canada--Biography.

Classification: LCC DS134.93.R38 R37 2024 (print) | LCC DS134.93.R38 (ebook) | DDC 947.085/2092 [B]--dc23/eng/20240315

LC record available at https://lccn.loc.gov/2024006078
LC ebook record available at https://lccn.loc.gov/2024006079

ISBN 9798887195124 (hardback)
ISBN 9798887195131 (paperback)
ISBN 9798887195148 (adobe pdf)
ISBN 9798887195155 (epub)

Book design by Kryon Publishing Services.
Cover design by Ivan Grave.

Published by Cherry Orchard Books, an imprint of Academic Studies Press
1577 Beacon Street
Brookline, MA 02446
press@academicstudiespress.com
www.academicstudiespress.com

Contents

Author's Preface

My father's story is not just a collection of memories and experiences; it is a testament to the strength of the human spirit, the will to survive, and the courage to face insurmountable obstacles. It is also a tale of coming of age, searching for belonging, and daring to escape an oppressive, tightly controlled Communist regime.

But for me, it is much more. As the daughter of a man who lived through such incredible circumstances, I obviously feel a deep personal connection to this story. When I was growing up, my father's accounts of his time in the Soviet Union and his subsequent near-impossible escape always left me in awe. But it wasn't until I convinced him to let me collect and write his stories—which sent me down a rabbit hole of researching the USSR after World War II through to Russia today and the Jewish experience in that period—that I put all the puzzle pieces together and came to a clear understanding of the magnitude of his journey.

I found it particularly fascinating to discover the strength and extent of the Soviet Jewry movement in the West in the 1960s and 1970s. This human rights campaign, which advocated for the right for Jews in the Soviet Union to emigrate, ran in parallel, historically, to my father's story. Through the Soviet Jewry movement, we saw the struggle of Soviet Jews mainly through Western eyes; only now are we hearing the voices of people—like my father—who experienced it from within. From his childhood misadventures in the days of Stalin to his increasing awareness of the paradoxes of the oppressive regime as he grew older, he faced his circumstances with a determination rooted in the constant hope that a better life was possible.

In sharing his story with me, my father untangled many of the complicated and sensitive issues that arose from being a Jew in the USSR. Strangely, a country based on an ideology that was supposed to bring the international proletariat together across ethnic lines and consigned religion to the dustbin of history required all its citizens to carry internal passports indicating their nationality—and for Jews, their nationality was marked "Jewish". Anyone carrying such a passport faced persecution, discrimination, limitations and petty harassment at every turn.

We see my father's family forced to reside in inhumane living quarters despite a promise of an apartment for my grandfather's role in liberating Berlin and his contributions as an officer in the Red Army during World War II. We feel my father's horror, at the tender age of eight, when he innocently shares with his teacher his knowledge that his classmate's family has been selling baked goods in a private marketplace, only to learn his honesty and good intentions result in this family's disappearance. We boil with frustration when we learn that if you applied to leave the country, not only would your application be denied, but you would be labeled a "refusenik," making it impossible to get any job. And then, in a touch worthy of Kafka, since it was illegal not to have a job you would be labeled a "parasite" and sent to the Gulag or a corrective labor colony, or assigned menial work in a remote area of the country.

And then there was distrust among the people, even among Jews. When my father initially tries to join the dissident movement and attends the only synagogue in Odesa to seek both belonging and a future, he is received with harsh skepticism from those inside and is terrifyingly harassed by the KGB on the outside.

I was raised under both the halo of my father's resilience and the long shadow of his traumatic past. I remember feeling a sense of pride and inspiration every time he shared his experiences and his staunch commitment to freedom with me when I was growing up. And yet, it would be impossible for me to even begin to understand his roots and routes without this undertaking of documenting his life. It serves as an entry point for a daughter to finally come to know her father, integrate the extraordinary mesh of his experiences—many familiar and some not—and meditate on the singular life of which I am an extension.

But beyond my personal connection, I believe it is important for all readers to learn of my father's experiences. The events that my father describes are not just a part of his personal history but also a part of the collective history of those who have lived under oppressive regimes. His story is a reminder of the human cost of political oppression and the sacrifices that people must sometimes make to protect their freedom. Whether you have personally experienced the challenges of totalitarianism or not, my father's story speaks to the power of human resilience in the face of adversity. In today's world, we are still grappling with issues of political oppression and the need for personal freedom. My father's story serves as a reminder that these issues are not just theoretical concepts, but real struggles that people are facing every day. Indeed, as I write this, such a struggle is playing out dramatically in the same part of the world where most of this book takes place.

I believe that this book also has value simply as a piece of literature. My father is a quirky storyteller. It is my hope that my account of his descriptions of life in the Soviet Union and his harrowing escape will keep readers turning pages, and his reflections on the meaning of freedom and the power of hope will remain with readers long after they finish the book.

Approaching his ninth decade, I was impressed by my father's sharp memory for the details of his early life as I documented his recollections; that said, I was equally amused to see him look back on his life and share in my surprise - we were both struck again and again by the improbable nature of so many of the events that led to his birth, his survival, his eventual freedom and even his later-in-life success. Perhaps most importantly, however, through our conversations he shared with me that he felt it imperative that the lessons he learned touch others. I couldn't agree more. Since my father's escape from the USSR he has continued to live a life of achievement, meaning, and sometimes adventure: fighting in the Yom Kippur War in Israel, completing his PhD studies in Israel and France and narrowly avoiding the Uganda hijacking of an Air France flight, moving to Canada and having a significant impact on the country's computer science advancements in practical settings (telecommunications firms, banks, insurance companies) as well as bringing his love of mathematics and problem solving to bright young Canadian minds. He has been an inspiration to me from an early age—and it was no surprise to anyone in our family that I followed in his footsteps and became an educator. My father and I worked together on our shared project, Brain Power Enrichment Programs, for many years, a project that would become Canada's award-winning and leading enrichment education provider for thousands of academically inclined students in first through twelfth grade. Our influence on Canada's future leaders has not gone unnoticed. Recently a (now former) CBC Radio host interviewed my father for a podcast where she wove together some of his USSR backstory with his philosophical musings on mathematics and genius-making.

I am thus honored to introduce my father's improbable life to you, in his voice. It is my hope that you will find it both inspiring and thought-provoking. His story, I believe, has the enduring power to touch the hearts and minds of readers. I trust it will resonate with you as much as it has with me.

Reuven Rashkovky's Preface

I think that from a young age my children suspected that their father's life story was beyond unusual. Given my mathematical background they came to appreciate the term "improbable" earlier than most - *something that can happen, but its probability is comparatively low* - and I suppose my existence is a living example of this definition. My daughter began collecting snippets of my stories the way other children would collect baseball cards or seashells - and eventually, as an adult, she convinced me it was time to document my arguably astonishing journey - a life that has been at the center of some of the most dramatic and tumultuous events in modern history. She assured me that, regardless of one's level of interest in history, readers would at least relate to the deeply human themes of hope, repression, disillusionment, triumph, and freedom found in my memories.

Certainly, on the one hand, my overall life trajectory has been somewhat similar to thousands of Soviet Jews of my generation - in this regard, it may seem to be not such an "improbable" life. But on the other hand, I witnessed and played an active role in various pivotal political events after WW2 - and the unlikely collision of surprising outcomes of survival is nothing short of astounding.

This record of my life forms a kaleidoscope of hardships and failures. There are successes, too – some earned by hard work and some received as a seeming "advance" for future sufferings. Altogether, when I observe the events, tied together, manifested from the realm of the possible to the realm of the realized, decisions made by myself, with my family, by nature/God/destiny, I see a life tapestry both unique and quite unlikely. Perhaps many people feel this way about their lives? I will let the reader, thus, decide how improbable my life has been, if at all. For myself, observing the panoramic view of my life, I am full of gratitude for all I have lived and experienced, despite the significant share of pain, horrible losses, and unwelcome surprises I endured.

In sharing my life events, I have attempted to be reasonably objective, at least, in splitting my life into particular "highlight" periods and did my best in this retelling. Of course, as with all retellings, we cannot escape ourselves, but I hope I managed to do passably well. All of the events and their chronology in the book are true, including people's names; note that some people's names are written in full (most often - but not always - it is for those who have already passed away) and others' names are shortened and include an initial for their last name (most often - but not always - it is for the privacy of those who are still with us at the time of this book's creation).

Finally, as those who know me will confirm, I can be quite opinionated on politics, religion, the field of education, areas of math and physics, and many other topics - but I committed to leaving out unnecessary opinions as much as possible for this book (admittedly, sometimes this commitment was upheld more than others). Emerson famously wrote that one's opinion of the world is also a confession of character - but I think this text is a window into my unusual life without muddying it with opinions.

Perhaps the book is a bit of a confessional for me, too, but I will end my musings here and let the reader simply enjoy a riveting journey from Soviet "paradise" to an unlikely freedom.

CHAPTER 1

In the Shadow of the War

My very existence is improbable. Most of my family had perished before I was born and it was through sheer, strange luck that I came to be. My parents were born (Mom in 1921, Dad in 1911) in Bessarabia, which is located west of the Black Sea, roughly coinciding with present-day Moldova, bordering Ukraine in the north and Romania in the south. Historically, various peoples have lived in this area: Turks, Germans, Ukrainians, Romanians, Jews, Greeks, Russians, Romani, and others. My father was from a small village called Shabo, on the Dniester River delta near the Black Sea, and my mother was from the village of Tarutino, whose population was half-Jewish and half-German. My mother completed only four grades of elementary school because of poverty, and my father finished seven grades before he dropped out to work. They weren't intellectuals, although they spoke several languages: German, Romanian, Yiddish, Hungarian, Ukrainian, and Russian.

At that time, Bessarabia belonged to Romania, and my parents moved to live in Ploiesti, Romania, after they got married (they met at a mutual friend's wedding). My father, a self-taught musician, learned to play violin and banjo and made a living playing in local orchestras after his official day job. It is amazing to think that his violin playing and obsession with music, which arguably caused us much grief at home, would one day enable his son, my youngest brother Izia (Itzhak), to become a Professor of Violin at London's Royal College of Music and be awarded a Fellowship by the Prince of Wales (now King Charles III) along with a number of invitations to Buckingham Palace.

With the rise of Romanian fascists around 1940, my parents fled from Romania but, as only hindsight would reveal, they chose the wrong direction. Instead of going south to Palestine or west to America, they ended up in Odesa, a lovely city on the Black Sea in the Soviet Union. My father later admitted that he was brainwashed by Soviet propaganda. The next year,

Germany invaded the Soviet Union, and he was drafted into the Red Army. Because of his useful knowledge of so many languages, he was almost immediately promoted to the rank of a junior officer. Assigned to the intelligence unit, he served as a staff officer in the division's headquarters near Odesa and helped with prisoner of war interrogation. The Luftwaffe often bombed the headquarters, and during one raid my father was hit in the leg by shrapnel and severely injured. Because he was an officer, he and his family were evacuated from Odesa to a military hospital in Andijan, eastern Uzbekistan. He spent several years in rehabilitation there, and eventually learned to walk again. In March 1945 he returned to his army unit and, while my mother remained in Uzbekistan, took part in the capture of Berlin.

I was born in Uzbekistan in November 1945. My mother joined my father in Berlin a few months after my birth, and I took my first steps there. My family's situation at the time was so terrible that my older sister had recently died of malnutrition. Before we went to Germany I came down with rickets, and my grandmother took me to an Uzbek village where locals cured me with camel's milk and kefir. We lived in Germany for about two years while my father served in the Soviet occupation forces.

My first memories are of 1948–49 in Belgorod-Dnestrovsky, a small city twenty-five miles southwest of Odesa where my father was sent to work for the police force. The city was still in ruins after heavy German bombardment. My family lived in one bedroom in an apartment that belonged to the family of a collaborator. After the Red Army liberated the city, a military court had sentenced the man to death. However, his wife and son continued living in a two-bedroom apartment, so the city authorities "generously" gave one of their bedrooms to my family.

Near the building's small backyard was a colossal shell crater. It was so deep that a few homeless people lived in dugouts at the bottom. I remember an old one-legged woman washing herself, and then her clothes, in the mornings at the bottom of the crater. In one of the other dugouts lived a man who had lost both legs in the war. I looked at them from our apartment above with interest, observing how they managed their tasks without the same number of limbs as most, but I don't remember feeling for them. Perhaps I don't recall my feelings. Perhaps we all were suffering. Perhaps I was too young for that at the time.

Reuven with his parents in Berlin, where his father was serving with the Soviet occupation forces, 1946.

Then one day, these victims of the war, along with others like them, disappeared. The craters and dugouts were empty. We had no idea what had happened to the disabled veterans of the war. Only recently have reports emerged that they were sent to remote areas because they didn't fit in with Stalin's celebratory vision of victory in the Great Patriotic War.

Everyone had difficulty finding food in those days. People had food stamps, but they were rarely enough. As a police officer, my father rode on his horse to nearby villages a few times a week. He would bring back a little bit of food from these excursions (bread, lard, dairy, homemade sausages and other such goods), but these extras were still inadequate for any sense of satiation. I felt enormous pride when my father and his fellow police officers rode along our street on their horses, passing by the building we lived in. My father's horse was white with grey and black spots, a beautiful animal in my eyes. My earliest memory of my mother's work is of a little farm on the city's outskirts, where they bred rabbits for food. After that, she started working in a fish cannery; she cut fish there for more than twenty-five years. During her fish cannery days, our main staple on the dining table was, unsurprisingly, fish!

When the government canceled food stamps, we could buy bread and other products in food stores. One day, when I was just shy of six years old, my mom gave me money to buy a loaf of bread before she went to work. I took my three-year-old sister, Hanna, by the hand and walked to the *gastronom* (supermarket) close to our home. There was a long line, but it was early in the morning and the store's doors were still closed. With money in one hand and my sister in the other, I navigated the forest of adult legs to get to the entrance. When the doors opened, the crowd frantically pushed into the store. I fell to the ground but wasn't trampled, fortunately. Eventually, I managed to get to the counter and bought the loaf of bread. Full of pride at having accomplished this difficult task, I had lost track of my other job: caring for my younger sister! With a feeling of dread I discovered that my sister was gone. I ran outside and looked everywhere, but couldn't find her. When they came home in the evening from work, I told my parents what had happened. My father contacted the police station and, by midnight, the police informed him that my sister had been found near the city's railway station half an hour before his call.

My parents forgave me. A few months later, my mom gave birth to my next sibling, Fima. In addition to taking care of Hanna when my parents were at work, I now had to take care of a newborn baby. In the summertime, he would lie in the zinc tub on the balcony almost all day long, and I had to see that no flies or other insects landed on him. I also had to ensure that his gauze diaper was dry (or changed when not), that he drank water and milk regularly, and that my little sister played with him within my line of sight. My six long years of life had certainly prepared me for such responsibility!

Shortly after my father was discharged from the police force, my family moved into a room in a two-bedroom apartment near the city center. By then, we were five—my parents and three children—all of us living in one room. In the other bedroom was an army officer and his wife, who had to walk through our room to get to their place. The officer was waiting for transfer to another city, and the city authorities assured my father that when he took up his post the whole apartment would be ours.

The day came when the officer and his wife had to move out, but another officer arrived to take their place. The broken promise left my father distraught. I remember him arguing, almost fist fighting, with the new officer for a few hours. The man went out and returned with a military patrol to help him move in. My father stood at the door with a heavy ax in his hands while we crying children stood behind him with my mother in defiant solidarity. When it got late, the military patrol gave up and retreated with the officer. From then on, until we emigrated to Israel some two decades later, we lived in that apartment on our own.

Because both my parents worked, my siblings and I could attend the state nursery and kindergarten. It wasn't bad—there was enough food, lots of kids to play with, and plenty to learn. The only bad memory I have is of consuming fish oil a few times a week; this was obligatory at government kindergartens. This happy, albeit short, period ended abruptly when I enrolled in the first grade of the elementary school.

Top Student—and Jew

My mother took me by the hand to the elementary school for registration a few days before September 1, the first day of the school year in the Soviet Union. The school secretary filled out a form for me by asking questions: my name, my parents' last and first names, their ages, our address and nationality. It was then that I learned for the first time that we were Jews. It struck me as another thing the adult world cared about but was irrelevant to me—the implications weren't clear yet.

My naïveté was short-lived. The first day of school arrived, and I was led into a classroom along with thirty-four other students. The teacher took attendance, calling each of us by our first and last names. When the teacher called my name, Riven Rashkovsky, the whole class started laughing. I was greatly surprised because nobody in the kindergarten had ever had a problem with my name. My first name definitely wasn't Russian and was very unusual in our small city.

During the breaks between lessons, and after school, the kids in my class made fun of me, pushed me around, and called me a "little dirty Jew." I was embarrassed and hurt, but I didn't know how to fight back. In addition to my "Jewish problem," I stuttered a lot, especially when the teacher called me to the blackboard. I remember standing at the front of the class, very stressed, feeling the floor swaying under my feet, and afraid that my teacher would say "Riven." I hated my classmates' laughter when they heard my name, and their taunting continued after school all the way home.

I wasn't a good student in my first year of school because of these problems and because my parents had no time to look after me. They worked very hard to provide us with the basics. After eight or nine hours of backbreaking physical work, they had no energy to check whether I did my homework or how good it was. Even if they looked at my homework from time to time, with their limited education they couldn't evaluate and guide me.

At one terrifying juncture, this situation shifted. When I was in second grade, my teacher visited our apartment to discuss my "academic progress" with my parents. She arrived at around 5:30 p.m. My mom was on an evening shift that day and was already at work. My father had eaten his early dinner and was resting on the bed, fully clothed, awaiting his evening work shift. As usual, after eight or more long hours working on a construction site as a bricklayer, he was scheduled to head to a restaurant at seven o'clock where he would play drums in a four-person band late into the night. Exhaustion was likely why, when the teacher came, my father stayed on the bed and listened to her complaints about me with his eyes shut and body in repose.

This seeming disrespect and lack of interest agitated her and she became more vociferous in her complaints. It got to the point where my father stood up and stepped behind our dining table, which stood in the middle of the room, to put some distance between them. She kept at him; and as she stepped forward, yelling at him and accusing him of neglecting me and my education, he stepped back. She complained about the quality of my homework, my poor handwriting, and my terribly low marks. She was a big, tall, and heavy Russian woman. When she began shouting at him, I was afraid that she was going to attack my father. Of course, she had to add that he, an uneducated Jew, *must* take better care of his children as they deserved a better life than his—but she had little faith he would follow through.

When she left, my father locked the front door, removed his thick, heavy army belt from the hook on the wall where it hung ominously, grabbed me by the hand, and started whipping me with the belt until I began bleeding. When he stopped thrashing me, he warned me not to tell my mother what had happened. Then he said that he would repeat the punishment if I continued bringing home low marks from school. He wouldn't accept marks lower than 80 percent.[1] How I was to attain marks above eighty was left to me. My stuttering worsened after this incident. I was afraid of getting low marks and being whipped by my father for it. Standing at the blackboard in front of my peers became a nightmare.

---

1   Soviet schools and universities used 1 to 5 grades rather than letter or percentage grades. However, for ease of reading, in this book Soviet grades were "translated" into percentages, common for North American readers.

This was far from being the only time my father beat me. He terrorized the whole family—he would explode if something wasn't to his liking and would often hit my mom and swear at her when he was drunk. Working on construction sites after being discharged from the police force, he started drinking heavily during the day at work and in the evening while playing drums in the restaurant. He would come home at midnight so drunk that he couldn't find his bed and sometimes slept on the floor, completely dressed.

And yet, I love my father despite all the abuse he inflicted on me and my mother and siblings. I know he sincerely cared about my schooling. He wanted to be a better human being and always worked hard to provide material support for the family. However, he had no education and no professional psychological support; he had lived a very difficult life through World War II, and he had made a huge mistake in fleeing from Romanian fascism and taking us to the USSR. I learned a lot from the negative experience of my father's behavior at home. I made a life commitment not to drink too much alcohol, to treat my wife and kids with love and respect, and to create a warm friendly environment at home—as much as I could.

After my father beat me for getting low marks, I realized that I had to learn how to learn. There were a few Jewish students in my class who always got high marks in most or all subjects. One of them agreed to let me do my homework at his place and help me out if needed. Step by step, I learned the craft of preparing homework, improved my skills in calligraphy, and even started reading books from the city library. My marks at school started going up. But sometimes I still got 50 to 60 percent on my assignments. On those days, I would run to my grandparents' apartment and stay there for a day or two until my mother came to take me home. By that time, my father would have cooled down and I would avoid physical punishment. By the end of second grade, all my marks were "excellent," which continued through third and fourth grades. Fear was an incredible motivator. I even started passionately writing short poems, but my strongest subject was math.

When I was in third grade, a new family moved into the apartment next to ours. Their last name was Kasyanov and they had a boy, Valeri, who was my age. He became my first best friend. I shared my first poems with him; we read books together and got into a lot of mischief, like sneaking onto a neighbor's garden to steal apricots, apples, and cherries. Valeri introduced me to fishing. His father managed a store that was exclusive to military personnel and his parents were friendly with my parents. Whenever Valeri's father went hunting, he would come back with some hares for my family—or better, he would make stew from the freshly caught game and share it with my family.

One very sad day, however, Valeri betrayed me: he sided with some boys who called me a dirty Jew. The pain was agonizing. I stopped talking to him and pretended that I didn't see him when he passed me. That is when I wrote my first pain-filled poem on the subject of losing a best friend at age eight (I've translated it from Russian below):

> Valeri and Reuven were two best friends,
> But this friendship was broken and came to an end.
> Valeri betrayed and broke all my trust
> So now he's been punished by me, and I simply must
> Not talk to him, not see him, and just pretend—
> Until all the pain in my heart will come to an end.

Despite the misery I felt at the time, looking back I came to see that all these little childhood hurts helped develop my resilience. Eventually, Valeri and I overcame our problems. I don't recall how we began speaking again, but we continued our friendship for another year until Valeri's family moved to a different city. Many years later, after the Soviet Union collapsed, I found him on the Russian website Classmates (equivalent to Facebook) and we exchanged some short notes about our lives. I never met him again, and I felt there was no point in keeping in touch. With me in Canada and him in Russia, I thought we were from two different planets when we reconnected, and we had little to say to each other when we did chat.

There were a few episodes from that time that I have always felt guilty about. One such moment involved a friend, Kravits, in third grade. He was a nice boy, and we spent lots of time together. His family had an illegal stall selling perogies, which they had baked at home with the intention of selling at an unsanctioned kiosk in the city's marketplace. Sometimes I would go along with Kravits and his parents and help out at the stall. Unfortunately, the teachers at school were intent on indoctrinating us with communist ideals—and private enterprise was forbidden in the USSR. We were told time and time again that to be a truly good person in the Soviet Union we should inform the authorities if we suspected anyone of engaging in such dealings. Moreover, even as children, we were told that the Soviet Union was our real mother— we owed more allegiance to the country than to our parents, siblings, family, and friends. We were also told that if we didn't conduct ourselves accordingly, we would be suspected of treason—and that if we did tell, we would be treated well and honored. Looking back, to use a Russian expression here, they were "hanging noodles on our ears."[2]

When it dawned on me that my friend's family was involved in something antisocialist, I felt inclined to report them. The little eight year old that I was didn't quite understand the cascade of consequences that would follow. I thought that if I reported Kravits, his family would receive help ("re-education") and I would receive praise (for which I badly yearned, what with all of the taunting I continued to endure as a "dirty Jew"). Sadly, and predictably, things didn't quite turn out so well for any of us. Kravits's family disappeared. Reporting them to the authorities didn't win me anymore respect or protection or love. And when I realized that I had potentially endangered my friend and his family, a dark shadow of shame came to stay with me that I have yet to shake off.

I remember the day Stalin died. The city's streets had high snowbanks after a storm, but it was sunny and the scent of approaching spring was in the air. Large groups of people were standing around tall poles that were topped with speakers. Slow, sad music flowed down from above, and a man's voice was announcing the death of the great leader who was loved by all his compatriots. Many people were crying, others were standing solemnly with sorrowful expressions. I couldn't understand why people were crying and didn't know who Stalin was. The blend of honest sadness and masked relief made little sense to me, but I felt the tension.

At school we were all instructed to mourn. We listened to funereal music and the Soviet youth movement was called upon to stand to attention and salute the bust of Stalin. Many of my classmates were crying. My teacher was crying. Yet at home, in my own family, I wasn't heartbroken. Was there levity in our home after Stalin was gone? Nobody spoke about their hidden relief; perhaps it was because I was still a child or maybe it wasn't something my parents gave much thought to, given their round-the-clock dedication to earning meager wages just to feed us.

One day, my father took me to a local music school, hoping I'd study the violin. He could play the instrument, but he didn't know how to read music as he'd had no formal musical education. His dream was that his children would become real musicians. When I entered the school's auditorium, I saw a grand piano proudly standing in the middle of the large room and an old

---

2   To hang noodles on the ears (вешать лапшу на уши) is a Russian idiom that means to deceive someone.

teacher with grey hair sitting at it. The juxtaposition of the beautiful large piano and the decaying elder struck me.

I didn't have much time to think about it, however, because the old man ordered me to come closer so that he could begin his examination of my musical ability. He hit a key on the piano and asked me to sing it, then another key, and another. I had no idea how well I was doing. At least I wasn't stuttering! After what seemed like an eternity, he called my father over and told him that I would never be a good violinist, but that if he really wanted me to learn an instrument they would accept me as a piano student. My father, who for some reason had no respect for the piano, was very upset at this proposal and responded that "in the Rashkovsky family, the boys must only play the violin." It was my first and last day at music school. Another notch of shame was added to my belt.

My mom also took some interest in my studies, to the extent she could, and on one important occasion came to my rescue. In those days, students in fourth grade had to sit exams at the end of the year to be accepted into junior high in September. I received excellent grades in all subjects—except in mathematics. I had solved all of the exercises with no mistakes all year long. I even loved problem-solving. To show off to my classmates, I "cracked" one math problem on the exam quite quickly using the order of operations method, combining a few steps into one. My teacher didn't appreciate my strategy and only gave me 80 percent, saying that she hadn't taught us to solve problems like that.

Reuven (far left) with his parents and siblings, 1957.

My parents had very high expectations of me, and my mom was distraught over my math grade. The next day she met with my teacher, but she couldn't make her change my grade. The day after, she went to the board of education and met with the school inspector. When he—a mathematician himself—saw my work, he said that I should have received more than a 100 percent grade for producing a nonstandard, quick, and elegant solution. He overruled my grade and I graduated from elementary school with excellent scores in all subjects. Thank you, Mom!

Confronting the Bullies

The local elementaries sent their graduates to three high schools. The places were designated by number, and School Number 1 was closest to home. On registration day, at the end of August, many parents arrived at the school to register their children. Mine were at work, however, so I went to sign up all by myself. I had to provide the registrar with my name, age, and nationality, as well as the same information about my parents, what elementary school I'd gone to, and various other things. Religion was prohibited in the Soviet Union, but strangely, nationality in my case meant my parents' religion! It was one of the many, many paradoxes of Soviet life I would encounter.

I brought my elementary school certificate, my report card, and the completed medical documents I'd obtained from the town clinic—all were registration requirements. I also brought some mischief—mischief I felt was necessary if I was to survive the next stage of my education. I "corrected" my elementary school certificate by changing my name from Riven to Roman. I longed to blend in and Roman was a very typical Russian name. The forgery wasn't easy to do, but after some fancy penwork my certificate looked very legitimate. Unfortunately, the person registering me asked me to hand over my birth certificate to verify the rest of my information. When he asked my first name, I answered "Roman" and, with my eyes averted from his gaze, hoped I didn't look too guilty.

The man refused to register me without checking my birth certificate. I ran home, picked up my birth certificate, and started to panic. How would I explain that my first name was Roman when my certificate said Riven? It was then that an idea crossed my mind. Though it was a short-term fix that would inevitably cause me long-term problems, I ran with it. I took a bottle of ink and put a few strategic drops on my first name so it would be tough to read. With that, I completed my registration and started my new life as Roman Rashkovsky.

Becoming Roman brought me some relief in class: teachers called me by my new name and nobody laughed. However, a few bullies in the class still figured out that I was a Jew (my looks made it hard to hide the fact—I had a large, conspicuous nose and dark skin, unlike the pale complexions of most of my classmates). The bullies made my life unbearable during recess and after school. There were a few other Jews from elementary school in my new class, but the bullies loved picking on me the most. Maybe I seemed the weakest or the most upset by their mockery.

I was one of the best students in mathematics in class, and I told myself that the bullies were jealous of my skills. On math test days, the bullies would sit around me and demand that I give them the answers to the problems. On those days they weren't too hostile toward me, and I typically gave in and helped them out. But everything would go back to normal the next day. They would push me around, call me a dirty Jew, and kick me—and all the while nobody in the class would come to help me or stand up for me. I was one of the youngest (my birthday being at the end of the year) and the second shortest, and I had no muscles to fight back. I was always hungry, too, and it showed.

The only advantage I had was my cleverness, but that wasn't enough. I had a burning desire to develop the physical strength needed to get the bullies off my back. In sixth grade I signed up for after-school track and field, but I had no success. I couldn't run fast enough for the coach to notice me; I was no good at the high jump or long jump because my legs weren't strong enough, and I didn't have the stamina for distance running. Moreover, I was still pretty hungry most of the time. After six months without progress, I dropped out.

But the idea of becoming stronger so that I could keep my tormentors at bay made me look for another answer. That year the school moved into a new four-story building next to the old one, which became a night school for working youth. The new building had a large auditorium and a well-equipped gym on the top floor. One evening I wandered into the gym. A group of young men, soldiers from the military bases in the city, were training on the parallel bars, the rings, and the high bar; they were doing vaults and performing routines on the pommel horse. These guys had huge muscles and broad shoulders and did fantastic exercises under the supervision of a coach, a sports teacher at our school. I sat on the bench in the corner, waiting for practice to end.

I approached the coach and asked him if I could join them and learn gymnastics. He asked me to show him my biceps, as he suspected I was too skinny, and then told me my muscles were almost nonexistent. He said that I could hurt myself, even break bones. I was distraught and started crying, begging him to take me on. He saw my determination and asked me to run to the mat on the floor and do a forward somersault. I gathered all my strength, ran, jumped in the air, did a somersault, and landed right on my tailbone. It was so painful! However, I didn't show my agony and asked the coach once again to let me join the team. This time he said yes. It was a vivid demonstration of the power of determination—a lesson that would help me later in life time and time again.

I would go to training on schedule three or four times a week, and I made it my mission to learn men's gymnastics. It was excruciating for the first few months, but I never complained as I knew practicing would help me solve my trouble with the bullies in my class. After each session, I would eat whatever I could find at home and visit my grandparents to eat some more; my growing muscles needed lots of food. I would also go to my friend Vova's home (more about him later) whenever it was appropriate in the hope of getting tasty high-calorie food. By the end of seventh grade, I had fairly visible muscles on my arms and shoulders. And I became a member of the school gymnastics team.

By spring, toward the end of the school year, I participated in a citywide competition for juniors as a member of the school team, which was held in our gym. Of course, as expected, almost all of my classmates came to see the competition. I took part in competitive exercises on the parallel bars, then on the high bar, and eventually some acrobatics on the floor; afterwards, some of the bullies came up to me, touched my biceps, and congratulated me. I won first place in these competitions in my age group and, for the first time, felt I could deal with threats from my schoolmates.

The first opportunity came the next day. I was standing in class talking to Vova, who sat at my table. Two boys passed me and pushed my head toward the table. I didn't flinch and immediately pushed them back quite aggressively. They stepped back, peering at me with curiosity, and one of them exclaimed, "Look at him! He showed some strength!" And then they just magically left me alone. From that day on, physical bullying against me largely stopped, although I did face another incident when I was in tenth grade.

There were two blocks on the central street in Belgorod-Dnestrovsky where people would walk on warm Friday, Saturday, and Sunday evenings.

Once when I walked there, five or six guys, including some of my class-mates, suddenly surrounded me and ordered me to walk with them to the park, where a few more of these thugs were gathered. One of the leaders, Anatoly K., asked me if it was true that I'd spoken about them disparagingly at school, calling them bullies. I answered that this was correct. Suddenly I felt a serious knock on my jaw; Anatoly had kicked me in the face. I jumped at him to fight, but the others surrounded me, leaving Anatoly outside the circle. I realized that I was trapped. I sat on a rock, covered my head with my hands, and told them that I wouldn't fight all of them at once. If they decided to beat me up, I wouldn't respond to them, but I asked them not to kick me in the head. They stood around me for a few minutes and decided to leave me alone. One of them said he would beat me up if he heard me saying something bad again. But the other type of torment, the antisemitic type, continued. This unfortunate and oppressive force continued to come at me in all areas of my life: from classmates, from teachers, on the streets—from what seemed like everywhere.

We had a very talented math teacher, David Zinovievich Knobelman. He was a mild-mannered, quiet, and polite single man who always came to class in the same navy blue suit and had lots of patience. I liked every lesson with him, and I learned a great deal. He invited me to his after-school courses, where he prepared us for the citywide math Olympiads. I was particularly good at two-dimensional and three-dimensional geometry. David Zinovievich became my role model and he prepared us very well for competitions.

I won the city's math Olympiad and had to participate in regional con-tests in Odesa. Two days before I was to travel to Odesa, David Zinovievich called me into the teachers' staff room. He said that the school's Olympiad committee had decided to send somebody else to Odesa. I understood that David was on this committee and that he'd been part of this decision. The news made my heart fill with incredible anguish. I felt hot tears of shame and disappointment well up in my eyes. David then told me that Viktor Grudachev—one of the bullies from my class—had been chosen instead of me because he wasn't Jewish. David tried to tell me, in a voice that was any-thing but authentic, that perhaps I would have the opportunity to win next year's competition, but he disgusted me. I ran from the staff room to hide my grief. Never again did I go to after-school mathematics or take part in math Olympiads.

In eighth or ninth grade, I participated in another citywide gymnastics competition. I was becoming very good, particularly on the parallel bars and rings. However, the jury awarded first place to a boy from another school. Their decision was evidently unfair: even my trainer told me that I was much better than the other boy. But the other boy wasn't Jewish. I was very hurt by this echo from the past, when I wasn't allowed to participate in the regional math Olympiad. To deal with the pain I decided that I had to be so much better than my non-Jewish competitors that it would look ridiculous for juries to not give me first place. I still had hope that the time would come when merit would win the day.

Discovering New Ideas

When I started at School Number 1, there was a tall boy among my fifth-grade classmates; he was more than a head taller than I. Vova (a nickname for Vladimir) came from another elementary school. He never bullied me, and he was an excellent student. One day I approached him and offered my friendship. I told him that since he was the best student from his elementary school and I was the best from my school, we might find many things in common. He agreed and invited me to his home after school. There I learned that he was the only child of a retired lieutenant colonel in the Red Army and a stay-at-home mom. The three of them lived in a three-room apartment with a separate kitchen and many books on the shelves. All of this was very different from my home.

We ate lunch together at his apartment. Wow, his mom was an excellent cook! For the first time in my life, I ate lamb and Olivier salad (a Russian version of French potato salad with chopped hard-boiled eggs, cooked green peas, small pieces of smoked meat, and mayonnaise). But the greatest surprise was the apple pie and a nut cake with homemade cream on top. All of these were exotic foods to me; I never saw such food at home. Vova's mom put the food on the table in the kitchen and left us to eat alone. I noticed that she gave me a stern look a few times—likely because of my lack of table manners, but this didn't bother me. After the meal, Vova said that he had to do his homework and his mom would supervise him—alone. I had to leave.

I was ashamed to bring my new friend to our apartment because I realized that we were socially way below Vova's family. A family of seven people, two parents and five children, lived in two rooms, each about 250 square feet. One room was our parents' bedroom, and the other served as a bedroom for five children, our living room, and our dining room. We had no water in the apartment and no toilet. There were two large beds on which my two brothers and two sisters slept head to toe. As the oldest child, I had a small trestle bed beside a brick stove.

There was an outhouse in the backyard and a smelly bucket sat between the doors in a short hallway in our apartment for night needs. Before my parents came home from work, I had to bring two buckets of drinking water from the water pipes about three hundred feet away from our house. In the evenings, before going to bed, we would wash our feet, and Mom would wash our socks for the following day. My parents covered our square dining table with an oilcloth. Mom would leave a little money under the oilcloth for each of us to take to school to buy a bun or doughnut for lunch. I was responsible for taking my siblings to kindergarten and school.

Since we had too many people in this tiny apartment and my mom was seldom home during the daytime, the apartment wasn't always clean and tidy. After school, my first task was to go over our floor with a broom and run to a nearby restaurant with a pot to buy soup or borscht before my dad returned home from work to eat his lunch. After lunch, he would go back to work and I could do whatever I wanted. On warm days I would head to the banks of the Dniester River to fish or catch crayfish. On lucky days I would bring home fish that I'd caught and prepare it for my parents; or my neighbors' kids and I would go on an expedition to "harvest" some fruits from people's backyards or the orchards on collective farms. These I would also bring back to share with my siblings and parents. Despite having a life very different from Vova's, I still did well in math, essay writing, geography, and other subjects—except sports and music. I didn't have to try hard to receive high marks.

When Vova invited me over, I started perusing the books in their library. The first one that impressed me was *Stories and Myths of Ancient Greece*. That pushed me to join the city library and read books on ancient Greek mythology and culture. The old librarian noticed that I was taking home two or three heavy volumes and returning them a week later. She asked me on several occasions if I really read these books so quickly. I told her that reading occupied almost all my time after school.

Over the next couple of years, in his parents' library, Vova and I discovered Russian translations of books by Edgar Allan Poe, Luigi Pirandello, Sherwood Anderson, Erich Maria Remarque, Ernest Hemingway, and other Western writers I'd never known before. Vova's home became a new place for me to read. Unlike what we learned in school, these books were free from Communist Party propaganda and boring Soviet patriotism. There was a feeling of freedom in reading these pages and imagining life beyond the Soviet Union. I read books about real people, their emotions, and fundamental human struggles. We immersed our young minds in the different worlds of faraway people, and we contemplated contemporary philosophy and new ideas.

We read many books on the shelves in Vova's apartment, discussed unfamiliar concepts, and step by step arrived at quite vehement anti-Soviet views. I trusted Vova and didn't hide my growing opposition to the ideology instilled in us through Soviet literature, history, radio, and newspapers. We knew it was dangerous to talk about these sentiments. Sharing such ideas with each other was reasonable, but still risky. We certainly didn't want anyone to find out about our views and fall under the scrutiny of the KGB.

At Vova's parents' we also found old, forbidden poetry books—Osip Mandelstam, Marina Tzvetaeva, Sergei Yesenin—and two volumes about the Bolshevik Revolution and Russian Civil War written by the Jewish writer Isaak Babel in the 1920s. I cannot overstate just how much we enjoyed reading and rereading the newfound poetry and prose, as beautiful and sweet as romantic music. We learned by heart all of the short tales from Babel's book of *Odessa Stories*; we adopted Odesa slang and used expressions that were witty and as sharp as surgical knives. All of this self-learning was the complete antithesis to anything literary we were taught at school. I was so thankful to have Vova!

In eighth grade, Vova became sick and was sent to a sanatorium for a few months. The doctors found dark spots in his lungs, tuberculosis symptoms, and he had to undergo some treatments near the Black Sea. I found out about this from his mom when I came over to their place two weeks after he had gone. His mother didn't tell me the name of his sickness or exactly where he was. A month or two after Vova had left, I received a letter from him. When I opened it, there was only one page with one word on it: "FRIEND?" The return address was on the envelope; I used this opportunity to write him a promise to visit him. I felt so much guilt for not contacting him for such a long time!

I saved some money over the course of a few weeks to pay for the thirty-mile bus trip to the sanatorium. It was located near Odesa, overlooked the Black Sea, and there were lots of trees and flower beds. Five or six boys shared Vova's room. All of them had similar medical problems. They were reading interesting books, listening to modern music, and drinking wine whenever some of them managed to escape unnoticed from the sanatorium to buy a bottle (or more). It appeared to me that Vova was enjoying an interesting social life. I spent a few hours there and returned home by bus. Despite my visit and repairing our friendship, I still feel such guilt—even to this day—over that letter from him that only contained one word: "FRIEND?" I couldn't believe I had let my true friend feel abandoned by me.

Reuven (far right) with his friends Vova, Viktor, and Sasha, 1958.

Meanwhile, a new teacher, Mark Geizer, arrived at School Number 1. Only about five years older than us, he was assigned the duty of leading our chapter of Komsomol, the Soviet youth movement. Vova and I became friends with Mark when he discovered that we knew Babel's books and the poets of the period before and during the Bolshevik Revolution. We learned that he collected lots of exciting books written by authors and artists we were not aware of. He introduced us to the French impressionists and art history. Vova had a talent for drawing and painting, so he frequently went to Mark's home to look at his books. Our teacher became something of a mentor to us. We had many discussions about international politics, which he knew well. He carefully avoided internal Soviet politics, however; we didn't mind, though, because it was clear to us how dangerous it was to speak of these things at the time.

In ninth and tenth grade, a new physics teacher, Ilya Simkovich, arrived. He was a very good teacher and a musician as well. He organized a school band of six instruments—violin, cello, accordion, piano, drums, guitar—and two singers. As nobody in our school played guitar, I volunteered to be the guitarist. I could pretend to play because in the noisy band nobody could hear me. Moreover, I started getting quite a lot of respect from my classmates and the audience for simply appearing on stage!

Besides this rock star hobby, it was because of Ilya Simkovich that I got involved in a deep study of physics. It was very different from working on math with David Zinovievich, and my physics interest compensated for dropping out of the extracurricular math classes. At that time, my interests revolved around gymnastics (three or four times a week), physics, reading (likely banned) literature outside of our school curriculum, and forbidden discussions with Mark Geizer on philosophical topics, politics, and women. He was older, very experienced, and had many exciting stories about "the world out there" and, admittedly, his sex life.

In the Soviet Union, all students and workers were forced to participate in the celebrations of the October Revolution, which, because of the calendar change after the Bolsheviks took power, was on November 7, and Workers' Day on May 1. The local Communist Party authorities organized massive parades: for many, many hours, people filled the streets waving enormous red flags and giant banners that declared the greatness of the Communist Party and its leaders. Two weeks before the parades, we had to prepare our own banners at school, refreshing the old ones and making new ones. Six ninth- and tenth-grade boys with high marks in all subjects, who also had some writing and painting skills, were selected for this task. We were given old banners and new canvases; paints and brushes were spread out all over the floor in the gym on the fourth floor. After talking about our tasks with the teacher in charge, we were left alone, locked from the outside to prevent other students walking in and disturbing us.

When we'd worked for a few hours, we became hungry and wanted to get out and buy food. The only way out was to open the window close to one of the building's corners and walk on the ledge outside, holding the drain gutter from the window in the gym to the open window in the hall-way. And this we did, six stupidly brave kids taking a chance. We climbed out during recess; it was noisy outside because many kids were in the playground. As we walked along the ledge, one by one, the noise stopped and a lot of students and teachers stared up at us from the playground and lower windows. Luckily, we all ended up in the hallway unharmed. A teacher suddenly appeared and immediately took all of us to the principal's office. How he yelled at us! He suspended us from school for a week, and he requested that our parents come in for a meeting with him and our teachers. When my mom went to the meeting and the teachers showed her where we'd risked our necks, she fell—completely unconscious—on the staff room floor.

The next time I was suspended from school for a week, it was for dancing to rock 'n' roll music. In those days, rock 'n' roll was called "American propaganda" and prohibited. We were not allowed to dance to it or listen to it, and we certainly couldn't own records. However, our friend, Valera Yudin, had somehow managed to record some songs from Western radio stations—they were Elvis Presley's hits and they were amazing. On some Friday evenings we had dance parties in the gym. Usually, teachers supervised these parties to ensure good behavior. We danced to music approved by our principal.

One evening, the supervising teacher left us for a few hours as he had many exams to mark. He was sitting in the teachers' staff room on the third floor while we socialized and danced. Valera was the DJ, and he used this opportunity to play rock 'n' roll. Vova and I demonstrated how to dance to the music using some acrobatics and crazy moves (we just made it up and had no idea what we were doing). Suddenly, the music ceased because the school principal, Alexander Ogorodnikov, had entered the gym as we were doing the dance demo. He pointed at Vova and me and ordered us to come down to the office with him. He announced that both of us were to be suspended from school for a week for dancing to Western, capitalist, rotten, decadent, prohibited rock 'n' roll. My parents were not notified about this punishment, thankfully, so I spent the week reading Vova's parents' books.

In those years Vova and I became friends with a boy, Boris, one year younger than us. He was interesting and intelligent, liked modern music, and was cynical about the ideology we were all exposed to at school. Basically, he was like us. We shortened his name to Bob and the three of us became a peaceful "gang." Valera Yudin became the fourth member of our gang because he could build radio recorders and tape modern music, and because he was cynical about the ideology of communism, too. Valera was humpbacked, but this never bothered us; he was a full-fledged member of our group. Boris's father was the head of the military hospital in our city and, through Boris, we had access to medicinal spirits that we'd drink.

On some Fridays our school had no party. On those mischievous evenings the four of us would invite four girls from another school to a private party. The first time we did this, we decided to randomly choose one girl each to avoid unfriendly competition and any bad feeling among us. Each girl's name was written on a piece of paper, we put the four names in a hat, and then we drew. I got Jenia (short for Evgenia), a little blonde girl two years younger than me. She was the least attractive, and I wasn't particularly excited about her; but I had to keep to our agreement. So, we listened to music, danced, drank some alcohol, and enjoyed the evening. At the end of that first party, I walked Jenia the short distance to her home. Before she went inside, we kissed. That was my first kiss. I felt that she was attracted to me, but I didn't have any reciprocal feelings.

Over time, I became more comfortable with Jenia; she invited me over to her parents' one day. Her father was a big boss—the head of the city's council. He looked at me with a bizarre expression on his face—an expression I immediately recognized. It was the same antisemitic look that greeted me on the streets and on buses from strangers who were clearly not Jewish. Her father ensured that I never stepped inside their house again. Sometime later, when Jenia was more open with me, she told me that her father had been terribly shocked that she had befriended a Jew. That incident put a wall between us and meant that Jenia and I would only be friendly with one another during parties and impromptu walks with friends by the river. Our relationship completely stopped when I started my studies at university.

School creative writing assignments and personal reflections were anything but that: they were not meant to be truly creative and were certainly not meant to prompt any real reflection. I dreaded writing essays in literature class and made an effort—even to my detriment—to avoid them, because I couldn't produce what was expected of me. I felt that it was much too inauthentic, despite the consequences. I could write a critical analysis of a novel, but I couldn't limit my analyses to the political views prescribed by the Communist Party that my essay was supposed to include. I always got high marks for grammar and low marks for my ideas, and the teacher often reprimanded me for thinking outside the Soviet box.

To avoid writing, I learned how to get a physician's note and avoid class. I would concentrate on all the terrible pains of being bullied and the shame of being on the receiving end of antisemitic remarks, and in so doing I would build up heat in my body. I forced myself to get a fever; in twenty or thirty minutes, I could get my body temperature up to about 100°F. I would visit a school nurse or physician and get their permission to skip class.

One night before an essay writing day, I felt a pain in my abdomen that stopped by the morning. I decided to use it as a reason for missing school that day. I went to the clinic with the complaint, and they sent me to the hospital right away. I showed the doctors where it hurt—and it turned out to be appendicitis. I was hospitalized that day, and in the evening I was on the operating table. I heard the two surgeons discussing my situation, each of them sounding surprised and concerned by what they had found: nothing! One of them said that he didn't see any inflammation and the appendix looked very healthy. The other surgeon looked through my records and exclaimed that he knew my father from their village because they'd attended the same school. It seemed a banal thing to talk about while my abdomen was split open. Then he said that since I'd already been cut into, it made sense to remove my appendix anyway and not wait for another time, maybe a week, a month, a year later, when it would actually be problematic. The other surgeon agreed, and they completed the surgery. It took me a few months to recover, but I was happy not to have to write an essay. Yes, that is how badly I didn't want to deal with Soviet nonsense—I was willing to undergo surgery!

A Connection with Israel

My mom's family lived in Odesa before the Second World War; they all perished because the Germans killed her parents, her brother, his wife, and their kids. However, my mom's three older sisters left Bessarabia for Palestine in 1929 when my mom was seven. Since then, my mom hadn't contacted them or made any attempt to find them because it was impossible and dangerous in the Soviet Union while Stalin was in power. After Stalin died in 1953, though, the Soviet regime started changing. At the first opportunity, a couple of years after Stalin's death, my mom sent a letter to the International Red Cross asking them to help her find her sisters, who were likely in Israel. A year or two later, we received an initial letter from Mom's older sister, Zipora, that confirmed their whereabouts and gave a brief account of their lives in Israel.

My mom was thrilled and wanted to reply, but she didn't know how to write in Russian, Hebrew, or Yiddish. So, I became her amanuensis. She would dictate and I made an effort to write calligraphically so it would be easily legible. I often embellished a few words to make her words sound better, conveying my mom's thoughts as best I could. I wrote letters to Mom's sisters a few times a year through all the years up to university. We started getting some material support from Mom's sisters as well. We received small parcels once or twice a year—parcels with clothes, shoes, a tallit (prayer shawl) for my father, and other items. We also received a lovely sweater with blue diagonal lines that was just my size. Everyone at my school came to look and touch it when I wore it to a school party. I took good care of this sweater. When I grew out of it, my brother Fima took possession of it, and after Fima my little brother Izia. So, this sweater served the three of us for many years.

During my last period at high school, I continued to take care of my siblings. The seven of us, Mom and Dad and five kids, still lived in two rooms. One of my many responsibilities was to bring a pail of black coal and firewood from the basement in the wintertime. I had to start a fire in our stove before my parents came from work, giving my mom the opportunity to make our supper quickly before my father would go to his other job at the restaurant.

My mother usually came home with a few fish stuffed into her bra, smuggled from the cannery where she worked. The next day I had to take some of this fish to the fish kiosk at the marketplace. I would knock on the back door and a big woman would let me in. She would count or weigh the fish and give me the money for my mom. Then she would sell it at official prices and pocket the difference. I understood this bartering system well. Sometimes, my mom would ask me to take fish to another address to get butter in exchange. Somewhere else, I would receive meat for fish.

That was the unofficial barter economy, where people working in different factories exchanged things they took from their workplaces. Giving goods to children to deliver helped make it less suspicious. All of this black-market activity happened because people's salaries were so low that they didn't have enough to survive on. There was a common saying: "The government pretends that it pays people well for their work, and the people pretend they work hard." That is why most people in the Soviet economy worked on two levels: the official level, usually from 8:00 a.m. to 5:00 p.m., and then the unofficial, barter level, selling material "borrowed" from workplaces after hours. Wishing someone "May you live on your salary only" was a curse.

CHAPTER 2

Slaughterhouse to University

_____

Moving to the Evening School for Working Youth

I had long been told that I had to apply to university upon completing tenth grade. However, when I was in ninth grade, the Soviet government introduced a reform in the education system: we had to stay in high school through eleventh grade. One more year was added to keep us at school.

In the spring of my tenth-grade year, Mark Geizer came to our home late one evening. After drinking tea with my parents and me, he told us about a schoolteachers' meeting. The school principal had announced a decision not to give me a favorable reference for my university application. This decision would be recorded on my high school diploma and render me unwanted by any university in the Soviet Union. The principal had explained that the teachers in our school had accumulated a lot of evidence that I wasn't a fan of the Communist Party and wasn't happy with my life in the Soviet Union. It was particularly evident in the many essays I had written (when I wasn't excusing myself to have a surgery), questions I'd asked in class about the inequality of life in the Soviet Union, and my fascination with Western literature. In short, the future denial of university life for me was because of my anti-Soviet outlook. This news cast a terrible shadow over my future. The four of us discussed my options. The only path Mark saw for me was to quit school and sign up for the night school for working youth. Nobody knew me there and I could start afresh.

In the spring of 1962, then, I began looking for a job. I was only sixteen and I had no particular skills or profession. During my first month of searching, I was desperate: nobody would hire me because of my age. One day I was talking with a guy who was two years older and working days while learning at night. He told me that the slaughterhouse on the outskirts of the city always needed strong workers. I went there, and they hired me, starting

July 1. On the last day of June, after receiving my tenth-grade certificate, I went to work. A few days later, I asked human resources to give me a letter certifying that I was working, so I would be able to sign up for night school. Much to my relief, I got what I asked for.

Reuven (left) with Mark Geizer, his teacher, mentor, and friend.

That summer was sweltering. I did a few tasks in the slaughterhouse: I was first put on a conveyor line to cut off the diaphragms of slaughtered pigs before they were cut in half and moved into a freezing facility. Our pay was based on our productivity, so the men were intent on killing more pigs during each shift. Thus, the conveyor line moved fast; there was no time to relax. And to stop the line would bring yelling and cursing down on whoever was causing the delay. I found the work physical, intense, and very difficult. The first few days I was devastated: much as I had during my first year of gymnastics, I ached in every muscle in my body. Though I was usually selected to work on pigs, the slaughterhouse also dealt with cows and sheep. When not working on the conveyor line, I would be sent to the freezer facility. There, the work was a bit easier: I had to load frozen pigs, sheep, or cows into railway cars or big trucks with freezers.

The working conditions were as difficult as the job itself. There was an army of giant rats running around when the conveyor was operating. They would run on top of my boots, between my legs, and even on the top of the conveyor itself. They disappeared, however, when the line stopped moving. The rats were large and incredibly smart animals—they certainly knew when they could run freely and when to disappear. There were lots of big dogs and cats around the place, and I noticed that some had no ears and many had scars on their noses and legs. The older workers explained that their injuries were the result of fights with the rats.

The best part of my job was access to the slaughterhouse's eatery. There was delicious borscht (Ukrainian soup with cabbage, beets, potatoes, and meat) at lunch. I had never eaten such meat at home! One day, I spoke with the guy who had suggested that I look for work at the slaughterhouse, and he explained to me that everyone there was taking a piece of meat home, and he demonstrated how it was done.

In my naïveté and desire to make my mom and siblings happy, I decided to follow his advice. I hid about a pound of quality meat in my overalls, took it to my locker, and stashed it in my boots. But as I was leaving that day, my manager appeared and asked me what I was hiding. He went directly to my boots and pulled out the meat that I planned to take home. He told me that we were going to the office immediately to fill out a special form that would document that I'd been caught stealing meat. I would be fired, passed onto the police, and maybe even jailed! I realized that this would be the end of my dreams of university and that any public knowledge of me thieving would shame my family. I started crying, begged him to forgive me, told him that this was the first time in my life that I had stolen, that my family was very poor, and that I had simply wanted to help them a bit. In the end, the manager softened and told me to go back to work and never try it again. From that day on, I never took anything from my workplace.

But the experience made me realize how much risk my mother was taking by bringing fish home from work. When I talked to her about it, she explained to me that she never took fish only for herself. Part of what she was taking from the factory she gave to the guards who searched workers on the way home. Sharing fish with the guards protected her—except on those days when the police would replace the guards. But on those days, the guards would tell her in advance not to take anything. Such was the system in the Soviet Union: everyone played their part in taking from the workplace.

July passed quickly, and in the second part of August I was sent to work where cowhides were stored. Unfortunately, I picked up fleas that were living on the hides and brought them home. My mother was hysterical when she found out that our beds had become infested with fleas—fleas which had bitten us all. She instantly removed all of the bedclothes and washed them by hand multiple times. She disinfected our clothes and all the beds. Then she declared that I wasn't to work at the slaughterhouse anymore—or else! But I needed a job to get my high school diploma and I implored her to let me continue. She told me not to worry: she would pull some strings with her connections and find a respectable job that would provide me with the papers I needed for night school.

Two days later, she gave me an address and asked me to meet with a Jewish man. He was the manager of a small construction company, and he took me on as an apprentice to a group of electricians. It was very close to September, when the school year would begin. Our team worked on the construction site of the city's new theater during September, October, and November. My father also worked at the same site; he was a bricklayer and stucco specialist. Sometimes we would work near each other, but we seldom talked. My task was to prepare walls for electrical wires. I used a hammer and chisel to make indentations in the walls where the cables would go. Sometimes I was allowed to put electrical lines into these channels by myself. I learned how to plan complex wiring schemes, read electrical drawings, install electrical panels, and so on.

As the winter temperature went down to a deep freeze, our team was sent to farms near the city to install electrical poles to bring electricity to newly built agricultural facilities. Our task was to dig holes in the ground for the wooden posts. The soil was very hard by that time, and we had pretty primitive tools—picks, crowbars, spades, and shovels. It was very windy in the fields and very cold. Our team had seven or eight people; most were tall, strong farmhands in their early thirties. They would dig the frozen soil for ten to fifteen minutes and then run into covered places to warm up and smoke. I was the youngest and I didn't smoke, so I had to stay behind and continue the work. After a few days of this, I realized that if I wanted to enjoy fifteen-minute breaks, I'd have to start smoking.

The leader of our crew was a city guy who was married and had two kids. By chance, we were in the same class in night school. He realized that I could help him with math, physics, and other subjects, so he looked after me at work and school. His aspiration was to get a high school diploma and study at the fishing technology college in our city. And I helped him to achieve this. His college entrance exams were at the end of May, and these were held in the classrooms on the ground floor. The end of May is warm, and most of the windows in the college were open to let in fresh air. My friend sat at a table close to one of the windows while I stood outside. He managed to pass me math problems to solve; I put solutions on the window sill when the teacher wasn't looking. We did the same in the physics exam. He got 80 to 90 percent in these subjects and was accepted to the college. We celebrated at his apartment with lots of vodka and tasty food.

Wintertime was very hard on me because of the job I did during daytime combined with my night studies. My school work was relatively easy; the material in eleventh grade was similar to what we'd learned in tenth grade. However, I was out of the house at seven every morning and I got to bed after eleven at night. The days were long and tiring, so I had almost no contact with my classmates from high school. A few of my classmates from high school were in the same class as me at night school, but we didn't socialize much. We had different reasons to be there; some wanted to improve their grades so that they would have a better chance of getting into university. I had my own reasons.

In the spring, I had to decide which university I would apply to and what subject I would pursue. Soft disciplines didn't attract me; given my inability to hide my beliefs, they would be too dangerous. I decided to try the Faculty of Mechanics and Mathematics at Moscow State University (MGU). Many of my Jewish friends told me not to apply there because its quota for Jewish candidates was very low (between 3 and 5 percent).[1] I felt that I should try my luck anyway. The entrance exams were scheduled for July; exams for other universities in the Soviet Union were in August. My idea was that if I failed in Moscow, in August I'd have a second chance in Odesa or another large city. I got my hands on some MGU entrance exam samples and books in March and started working on preparing for July. So did my friend Vova, who was the best student in the day school. Sometimes we studied the exam material together—mostly on weekends, as on weekdays I had to go to work.

By the end of May 1963, I realized that I would need a passport[2] to go to Moscow to apply to university. I ran into a problem when I applied for a passport at the city's police headquarters. When I produced my birth certificate with lots of ink on my name, the officer told me that it wasn't valid

---

1   On Soviet antisemitism at universities, see Tanya Khovanova and Alexey Radul, "Jewish Problems," October 18, 2011, https://arxiv.org/pdf/1110.1556.pdf or http://www.tanyakhovanova.com/coffins.html, or Jay Egenhoff, "Math as a Tool of Anti-semitism," The Mathematics Enthusiast 11, no. 3 (2014): article 11, https://scholarworks.umt.edu/cgi/viewcontent.cgi?article=1320&context=tme.

2   In the Soviet Union, every citizen over the age of sixteen had to have an internal passport which contained information about them and their parents, nationality/ethnicity, a stamp from local police saying where they lived, and so on.

and that he couldn't issue me a passport. I was advised to write to the birth registry in Andijan, Uzbekistan, and request a new, valid copy of my birth certificate. So, I had two issues at hand: (a) it usually took more than three months to get a response from Uzbekistan and I needed it in a month, before July; and (b) even if I could get a new birth certificate in time, my name would be Riven. On all my school papers, by that time, my first name was Roman. I felt that I'd built a trap for myself by changing my first name—and not very legally.

With this headache, I again went to Mark Geizer for advice. I explained my situation to him and asked if he could help me, given that he was friendly with a few guys in the police department. A few days later, he met me and said that I could have a passport, but that we'd need a bottle of medical spirit or vodka and nice food to entertain the head of the passport-issuing department. My mom promised to help me out with this endeavor.

A few days later, Mark and a captain from the passport office showed up at our place. The captain brought a guitar with him. We were sitting at our dining table, eating plates of fish, and drinking spirits to the point when the captain took his guitar and impressed us with his vocal skills and guitar playing. My siblings were not at home and my parents were at work, so it was just the three of us. As the captain drank, he became more sentimental and started singing sad songs. When he'd had enough and was ready to go home, he hugged me and said I should come to his office in two weeks to get my passport. After that, Mark walked him home.

It was the end of the school year. There was no year-end celebration at the night school. We went to the school's office, and our classroom teachers gave each of us a high school diploma. In addition, I received a gold medal for completing high school with a five (excellent) in all my courses. I would never have got such a medal in the day school because the teachers there for subjects such as literature and history had never given me high marks; the decision had been made at the teachers' meeting a year earlier. Some of my old classmates from the day school came to my home and officially invited me to their celebration party (prom). I accepted the invitation. The party was in the auditorium on the fourth floor; my old teachers and classmates were there, as well as festoons of flowers and tables set with food and sweets. I felt like a stranger.

Entrance Exams at Moscow University

After the prom with my former classmates, I went to the passport office in the city police department. The captain was there. He gave me a strange-looking passport. A regular passport was green and small enough to carry in a pocket; the one I received had a cover made of light-blue cardboard and was much larger. I asked the captain what he was giving me. He explained that he couldn't provide me with a regular passport because of my damaged birth certificate; instead, he had given me a temporary one which would be sufficient to travel to Moscow for the entrance exams at MGU. He told me that, after the exams when I had some free time, I should write to the Andijan registry to send me a copy of my birth certificate—this would allow me to get a real passport.

I had no choice but to use this temporary passport to get to Moscow and register for the MGU entrance exams. I resigned from my job and used my last pay packet to buy a ticket for the Odesa-to-Moscow train and have enough pocket money for a month in Moscow. At the end of June 1963, my mom walked with me to the early morning ferry to Odesa. She asked me to be good and do well in my exams.

In two hours, I arrived at the railway station in Odesa, bought a ticket for a shared compartment, and sat on the train. It took about twenty-seven hours to get to Moscow. By chance or by luck, Vova and his mom were also in the same car—but in a separate compartment for four people. It was my first time being away from home for a long period of time. The train stopped at stations in northern Ukraine, where many women and men from collective farms sold sour cherries at very low prices. I bought a small basket of cherries and nice apples. Combined with sandwiches my mom had given me, I had sufficient food for my journey.

Upon arriving in Moscow, I first went to MGU to register for the exams; my high school certificate with my excellent marks was sufficient to register. I was offered, and readily accepted, a place in a dormitory during the exams. The registrar gave me a ticket and explained how to get to the dormitory. There I met the superintendent, a large blond woman. She asked me to show her my passport. When I gave her my temporary one, she looked at it, turned it in her hands, looked at me quizzically, then asked me when I'd been released from prison. (Apparently, this type of passport was usually given to recently released prisoners.) I explained what happened to me when I'd tried to get a passport and assured her that I'd request a good copy of my birth certificate to get real papers after the entrance exams. She accepted my story and assigned me a bed in a room with three boys who were in Moscow for the same exams. We had two days' introduction to the process: the location, the rules, and our rights should we want to dispute our marks. We then began our exams.

In 1963, acceptance into the math faculty at MGU was based on the successful completion of five exams: math (written and oral), Russian literature (written), foreign language (French in my case; oral), and physics (oral). The final grade would consist of five grades on exams and the average of my high school diploma grades (5 in my case). In 1962, candidates with a gold medal from high school had to write only one exam: math. I missed this by one year, but I still had an advantage as my average score was the maximum.

The written math exam had four problems in algebra and 3D geometry. I solved the first algebraic problem, then worked out a complex geometry problem. Somehow, I could imagine the proposed structure of the pyramid and crossing planes; I could see the solution for the complicated and challenging geometry problem. The third problem, algebraic, was tricky for me. I could write only one equation with two variables and didn't see how to solve this equation. This kind of problem is easy for me now, but I was stuck—I had never seen this kind of thing at school. Instead of solving an equation with two variables, I started guessing and checking the answer. By sheer luck, I landed on the solution. However, I had no time for the last problem.

Two days after the written math exam, the list of students that had failed was posted on the bulletin board. I had seen many students crying or upset and yelling when they found their names on the list. But I had passed! I went to the committee and asked permission to see my exam and the comments made by the person who checked my work. My first two problems were solved perfectly. The comment on the third problem was that the logic applied to arrive at the equation was correct and optimal. However, the way I solved the equation demonstrated that I didn't know how to apply the proper technique, and either I'd solved it by a guess-and-check method or, somehow, copied an answer from somebody. The comment was fair, and I didn't dispute it. Anyway, I passed the next exam.

I don't remember the math oral exam; it was routine, and I did well on it. However, the exam in literature was torture because the theme was "Happy life in the Soviet Union." Of course, by then, I knew what not to write; still, I couldn't write enthusiastically about the topic. Again, I passed that exam. I got a respectable mark on the oral French exam because, thanks to my high school French teacher, I was able to demonstrate my "Parisian" accent.

The fifth and final exam, an oral in physics, left me feeling dreadful. I had to choose one of many tickets lying upside down on a table. Each one contained a few questions on theory and three problems. I had half an hour to prepare, sitting at one of the desks in the room, not far from the professor. I knew how to answer the theoretical questions, and the problems weren't too complex. When my turn came, I sat opposite the professor and presented my theory. He never interrupted me, and I gained confidence. Then I explained to him my solutions to the problems. In the end, he said that this was enough and told me that he was giving me 3 (60 percent).

I was pretty upset and asked him why. He answered that my presentation was good, but felt that I didn't know some things. When I asked him what I didn't know, he shrugged his shoulders. I told him that a mark of 3 would prevent me getting into MGU and I asked him to give me a second opportunity. He agreed. I drew another ticket and spent another thirty minutes preparing the presentation and solving problems. Again, he never interrupted my presentation and never argued with my solutions. When I finished, he said that my mark would remain a 3. I looked into his eyes and saw that he had no intention of giving me a higher mark. At that point, I understood that I was regarded as undesirable: no matter how good I was, I wouldn't be accepted into MGU. I had finished one point below the entrance threshold.

When I came out from the physics exam, Vova was already waiting for me in the hallway. He informed me that down the hallway were a few tables with representatives from other universities eager to recruit candidates who had passed all exams for MGU but didn't have enough points to get in. Vova, too, hadn't got enough points for MGU. I went to see what was there and how it worked. There were representatives from three universities: Odesa, Tomsk, and Kazan. I considered only two—Odesa and Tomsk. On the one hand, Tomsk was in the northern part of Siberia—a freezing place; however, university students from Tomsk were not drafted into the army for the usual three years of military service. On the other hand, Odesa was very close to home and a warm place on the Black Sea; however, there was a good chance that male second-year students would be drafted into the army. I had two days to make a decision, so I called my parents for their advice. After a short discussion, they ordered me to choose the university in Odesa. I submitted my papers to the Odesa representative and took the Moscow-Odesa train. It was the end of the third week of July. My classmates, like most students in the

USSR, had to go through the application process in August. It was so lovely to come home to Belgorod-Dnestrovsky as a University of Odesa student while the others had pre-exam stress.

In my last two days in Moscow, I was out of money. There were two other guys still sharing my room, and they helped me with some food. We had excellent talks about literature, famous poets, and philosophy. In the evening, one of the university students ventured into our room and asked us if we would allow him to sleep on the empty bed. He also took part in our discussion. It was a night with a very starry sky. I tried to explain my view that our universe is only one layer of existence. Inside any physical body, there are atomic and subatomic levels mimicking our universe and, possibly, harboring some kind of life within. By analogy, our universe may be a tiny "atom" in a higher universe, which contains its own life. Now I understand that my belief in the similarity of atoms and our planetary system led me to that conclusion. The student who joined us said that my thoughts were not original. He told me that my view was a version of embedded-worlds philosophy—an idea entertained by quite a few people. Today, I know much more about matter and life and, like most of the scientific community, I am skeptical about my once strongly held convictions. But hearing the student's words was like having cold water dumped on my head: I abandoned my line of thinking, but I never forgot this experience.

My First Years at the University of Odesa

A week before September 1, 1963, the start of the new school year, I came to Odesa to register at the university and to sign into the dormitory. Standing in line for registration, I met a few of the students I had talked with at MGU. I was given a temporary student card and directions to the dormitory, which was four blocks away from the university's main building. In the dormitory, the superintendent asked me to present my passport. I once again had to explain why I had a temporary—strange, in other words—document. It worked. She sent me to a station to disinfect my belongings, shower with disinfecting water, and come back with clearance to live in the dormitory. It took me almost a whole day, but I had my bed in the dormitory room by the evening. Like the first one I'd stayed in, it had six beds for new students.

Vova didn't need a place in a dormitory because his parents rented a room for him not far from campus. When I visited him in the second or third week of September, three students from our math department were drinking wine and celebrating our status as new students. I joined them, and we emptied a few bottles of wine. Intoxicated, we decided to stroll on Pushkin Street. It was already evening. It was warm; few people were on the sidewalk. For no reason or to show off, I jumped and kicked and overturned a city garbage can.

We continued walking and talking loudly—until I noticed that my friends had disappeared some twenty-five to thirty-five yards from the overturned garbage can and a group of men wearing red epaulettes surrounded me. I soon discovered that they were a civic patrol composed of older students from various institutions. In those days, civilian patrols helped the city police keep the streets free from hooligans and prevent threats to the public. The leader of the patrol asked me why I had overturned the garbage can and demanded my passport or any other identification. I only had my new student card on me. They looked at it and said that they would arrest me, which would result in my expulsion from the university. At that moment, my head cleared and I realized that I was in deep trouble. My friends, who could advocate for me and save me from my predicament, had vanished. I started begging the patrol team to forgive me, and explained to them that I'd had a few glasses of wine and had lost my self-control. After ten minutes of pleading, the leader told me to return to the garbage can, stand it up, and put all the garbage that had spilled onto the street back into it.

It was humiliating to collect cigarette butts, dirty paper, and pieces of unfinished food—all of which was full of sputum and dust. I understood that this was my only way out of trouble, so I did what I was told—all the time hoping that the patrol would give back my student card. They watched me as I was cleaning the street of the mess I had created and, when I was finished, they told me to remember this evening and never repeat it. I promised and asked them again to forgive me and give me back my card. After they'd done so, I turned around to go back to my dormitory. Suddenly, as if out of nowhere, my friends reappeared. But I didn't talk to them; I was too upset and humiliated. However, I learned my lesson well: the events of that night were imprinted on my memory.

The next week we were taken for three weeks to a *kolkhoz* (collective farm), some forty miles from Odesa, to help harvest corn. We had a great time away from the city and the university's lecture halls. We were accommodated in villagers' homes. During the day, we worked in the fields; in the evenings, accompanied by a guitar, we sat around a fire singing student songs. I enjoyed that time.

I still didn't know how to learn properly, how to work, study, and succeed at a university level. I sat in on almost all of the lectures on higher algebra, calculus, drafting geometry, and other subjects, assuming that to do so would be enough. But I had a major shock in the first December exam: each student was required to randomly select a card on which were written some questions on theory and a few exercises. We sat in front of the professor in small groups, each of us at a separate table, and were given twenty to thirty minutes to prepare a presentation. While I was waiting for my turn to enter the room for my first exam (in algebra), I saw students who had completed it: I saw tears in the eyes of those who had failed or had received a mark much lower than they had expected; however, I also saw joy on the faces of those who'd succeeded. Looking at these students, I became nervous. I chain-smoked, realizing that I wasn't ready for the challenge ahead.

I was relieved because the theory questions on my card were easy, but I stumbled over one of the problems. Before presenting my work to the professor, I realized that I could use one of the theorems from my card to solve the problem. As I was answering his questions, the professor asked me a few related ones, and then he reviewed my solutions to the problems. But he didn't like my approach to solving the most difficult (for me) problem. He said that I'd "used heavy artillery to shoot at a small sparrow." He asked me if I was aware of a much simpler way to solve it, but I was too stressed to think about it anymore and started stuttering. He looked at me with pity, said that I didn't participate enough in practice lessons, and wrote 4 (80 percent) on my scorecard. I was so relieved; I had passed my first exam.

On the other three exams, my marks were lower—3 (60 percent). I was devastated by my performance in calculus, theory of limits, and continuity of functions. I realized that I didn't understand epsilon-delta language and its definition of continuity/discontinuity of functions. I lost self-confidence and wasn't sure if I would be able to do anything about it. I failed an exam on the history of the Communist Party and immediately signed up to try again later in December. I saw many students taking notes during lectures, which they used to prepare for exams. Vova lent me his notes from the history of the Communist Party lectures for two weeks. Reading them was torture for me. In the end, I got a mark of 3 and was happy that the first semester was behind me. With my low marks, I almost lost my place in the dormitory and my student allowance (about thirty rubles per month). I had to stand in front of the committee that supervised financial support for students and promise to improve my marks in the following semester.

I put more effort into my studies in the second semester, and my marks got a bit better: half of my results were 80 percent and the rest were 60 percent, So, I could count on a student allowance and a place in the dormitory for the next school year. During the summer, I found a job at a wine factory so that I could earn some money to buy some clothes and shoes for the new school year. My job was to load transport trucks with boxes of wine. This required muscles and endurance. I liked that.

As in my first year of university, we were sent to a kolkhoz during the first three weeks of September 1964 to help harvest corn. In October, some of the guys from my group received letters requesting them to appear at the army draft office. It felt inevitable that, by late fall, I too would be drafted into the Red Army. My strategy to avoid the draft was to stop checking my mail. When I saw an official envelope with my name on it, I would disappear from Odesa for a few days to visit my family in Belgorod-Dnestrovsky. I continued playing this cat-and-mouse game until late October.

Meanwhile, on October 14, 1964, there was a sudden change in the government. The party leader and the Prime Minister of the Soviet government, Nikita Khrushchev, was removed and replaced by Leonid Brezhnev. It didn't much change life in the Soviet Union, but it was indicative of the turmoil of the times. Khrushchev, when he visited the United States, was very impressed by the American farmers growing corn. Upon his return to Moscow, he'd ordered Soviet collective farms to grow more corn. As a result, the USSR hadn't produced enough wheat to feed its population. The wheat shortage led to the coup which had removed Khrushchev from power. In the student cafeterias, where bread was rationed, international students from Vietnam, East Germany, and African countries could eat white bread with their meals; regular Soviet students, however, were given only two slices of black rye bread. It was an absurd situation, underlining the discrimination in the Soviet system: we could all sit together at one table, but we were forced to eat different bread.

CHAPTER 3

Army Days

Becoming a Soldier

One evening in the fall of my second year at university we were sitting in our dormitory room playing cards. Suddenly the door opened and an army major stepped in and asked, "Who is Roman Rashkovsky?" The game stopped and everyone looked at me. "Aha," exclaimed the officer, "this is where you're hiding, you son of a bitch. Here's the letter for you; sign on this form that you received the letter. Tomorrow morning at nine o'clock you must report to the army's draft office. You'll be imprisoned if you don't show up." I was trapped; I could no longer run from the army.

The next morning I reported to the center, where I was told to be ready in three days' time to join a large group of newly drafted youth from Odesa. That same day, I took a bus to Belgorod-Dnestrovsky to visit my parents and siblings so that I could say goodbye before being conscripted for three years. It was excruciating. While there, I walked along the city's empty streets at night, saying goodbye to my childhood, to all good and bad memories. Most of my classmates from high school were away at university; I had no one to talk to about my fears.

After two days at home, my mom prepared me a bag with some food, gave me the little money she could, and I went back to Odesa. The small ferry that took me across the Dniester's estuary was fighting heavy waves as I looked at the contours of the old Turkish fortress on the cliffs above the Dniester, at the houses that I wouldn't see, probably, for the next three years. I had tears in my eyes.

In Odesa, I went to say goodbye to Vova. He told me that he wouldn't be drafted into the army: his mom had presented letters from various doctors stating he'd had tuberculosis in the past and that his lungs were still too weak to serve. He also mentioned that his mom bribed somebody in the drafting center, but he didn't tell me much about it. I was thrilled for him to be able to avoid three years as a soldier. The following day was the beginning of my army service. I was eighteen years old.

On the first morning, we had to surrender our passports, sign some papers, and, still in our civilian clothes, march to the railway station in a column, four boys in a row. I didn't want to give away my temporary passport; I told the officer that I'd forgotten it at my parents' home. He told me to write home, asking them to find it so that I could surrender it to my future commander. I promised to do so; however, I never followed through with the order.

We then were loaded onto a train, in regular passenger cars. By the time the train had moved away from the Odesa railway station, bottles of vodka were open, glasses filled, and we were drinking and eating food prepared by our parents. We didn't know our final destination and, after a few hours of drinking, we didn't care. By the middle of the second day, we'd run out of vodka. Some guys had weed to smoke; others drank small bottles of cheap perfume mixed with water. I couldn't do those things, and so for the rest of the trip, I only watched what was going on.

It would take three days to arrive at the city of Dniprodzerzhynsk (now Kamianske), on the banks of the Dnieper. And this would be the beginning of a phase of my life that would last three years. By the end of it, I would have witnessed an astonishing international incident and found myself in a uniquely uncomfortable military position—existential, really—during a crisis in Israel. To make matters worse, after I left the army I would see my dreams for the future collapse, and for the usual reason—because I was a Jew. But before all that happened, there were many mundane—although sometimes bizarre—details of army life to get used to.

We arrived in Dniprodzerzhynsk at dusk—still not knowing what to expect or what branch of the army we were joining. We were put into columns (as always, with four people per row) and a sergeant ordered us to march and sing a well-known military song. From the railway station, we trooped—still in our civilian clothes—to the army bathhouse. It was the end of October; the air was cold in anticipation of early snow.

Inside the bathhouse, we had to undress, put our civilian clothes into specially prepared bags, and surrender the bags to the sergeants. Then we had to pass a row of soldiers with haircutting instruments. We lost all the hair on our heads that night. We were given a piece of soap, and we proceeded to shower in a large room; it was very noisy and filled with awkward naked bodies.

After I finished washing and got out, I was given a towel, a stack of army clothes, and a pair of boots. Ten minutes later, I stood among young soldiers in new green army uniforms, complete with boots up to our knees. Looking around, I recognized friends with whom I had been traveling and drinking vodka for the past three days. We were put in a line and told that we were in Dniprodzerzhynsk to begin our training and learn how to service fighter airplanes. We were promised more information the next morning. We were led along the city streets to our base and into the dining hall. We ate our supper and afterwards were assigned beds in the barracks.

The next day we were split into several large groups. The commander of our group was Captain Kouchinsky. He explained that we comprised the better-educated soldiers and would learn the radio and radar systems of Soviet fighter planes. Other groups would be taught the mechanical, hydraulic, armament, and other systems of the various aircraft. He introduced our sergeant, our immediate boss, who'd see to our initial army training and needs. The sergeant answered our questions and, after half an hour, took us out for marching drills. Later, he showed us many other important military skills: saluting officers; completing our kitchen duties; caring for our beds, uniforms, and boots; preparing for morning inspections; and maintaining our rifles. He also taught us how to get out of bed at 6:30 in the morning and, within thirty seconds, make our beds, dress in our uniforms, and stand in front of our beds ready for inspection and regular morning exercises. Accomplishing those tasks so quickly wasn't easy for the first few weeks, but we improved with time.

Once we'd learned the rudiments of army life, we were tasked with becoming familiar with the Red Army's *Book of Laws and Penalties*. We discovered that straying outside the army's rules would lead to severe penalties—including the death penalty! About two months later, we were ready to swear fealty to the country and obey the orders of our officers and superiors—in times of peace and war. After signing our papers and pledging, we were full-fledged young soldiers.

Our barracks were on the hill overlooking the town. At the end of November, we had winter's first snowfall and the temperature dropped well below freezing. From the hill the city looked gray and gloomy, even when covered with snow, which was different colors—orange, blue, green, red, and so on—in different parts of the city. This was because the many factories spewed fumes of varying colors and stained the snow accordingly. Those of us who had begun our army service in October received permission to leave the barracks for five hours to spend time in the city. We arrived at the city center, which was crowded with sturdy-looking office buildings and supermarkets, but there weren't many people. As alcohol wasn't allowed in the barracks, our priority was to buy a bottle of vodka. We split into threes because a bottle cost three rubles; we each contributed one ruble.[1] We also bought bread and found a place between two buildings to drink. One at a time, we drank directly from the bottle and ate the bread, which was what most soldiers did with their free time. However, because it was cold and we could find nothing else to do in the city, we decided to return to the barracks an hour later.

In February, I got a letter from home that my mother was coming to visit me. I was given six hours off the base to spend with her. She was staying with the daughter of my night school chemistry teacher, a young woman who lived in a two-bedroom apartment with her husband in the military housing on the outskirts of Dniprodzerzhynsk. I remembered her from my school days: she was a gorgeous Jewish girl, a few years older than me, who had black curly hair, pale white skin, and beautiful blue eyes. She'd married a non-Jewish army officer and she was happy to help my mom and me. We spent a few hours in her apartment talking, eating lunch, and drinking wine. That evening, I returned to my barracks while my mom took a train back home, about 340 miles from Dniprodzerzhynsk.

Our days were repetitive: wake up at 6:30 a.m., make our beds and use the restroom (for which were given five minutes); complete thirty to forty minutes of morning exercises (such as running outside for a mile or two— which we did regardless of freezing wind and snow); stretch, shave, and clean our teeth; dress for the sergeant's inspection; and, finally, eat breakfast in a big dining hall. After breakfast, we sat in on officers' lectures on party directives, policies, and soldiers' responsibilities. We spent an hour marching in columns, learning to march in the style of the German army. By eleven we would be sitting in our classrooms, where my platoon studied the various fighter planes' electronics, radio, and radar systems. After lunch, we had another two or three hours of classes. After six each evening, we had a couple of hours to read books and prepare for the next day: wash our shirts (if it was

---

1   Assembling a group of three to buy a bottle of vodka, with each person contributing one ruble, was at the heart of Russian drinking culture. Often the three people would be strangers who communicated their interest in forming such a group through hand signals on the street.

the weekend), stitch a piece of white cloth to the collar of our green shirt (*ghimnastiorka*),[2] polish our boots, and cut one another's hair if needed.

One cold day, as we were marching around the drill square, Captain Kouchinsky called me to the classroom. The captain was alone when I showed up, and he made me a proposition. He said that, since I was from the second year of the university's math faculty, I was the most educated soldier in our platoon. He wanted to develop advanced teaching material for the radio and radar systems for Soviet fighter planes (MiG 17, MiG 19, IAK, and IL). He asked me to prepare slides on theory, diagrams, and system designs based on his notes. He explained that I would do this work instead of marching outside with our platoon during the winter months. I enthusiastically agreed to take on this project—without thinking about why I was offered such a sweet task. Honestly, I was relieved to be excused from stupid marching exercises in the cold.

From time to time, our officers organized sports competitions among our platoons. Once, it was wrestling. We had a few guys in different weight categories who demonstrated excellent skills. But the most exciting match was in the heavyweight category: one guy was clearly from a large city, well trained (at a submaster class) in wrestling; the other guy, from a village in western Ukraine, was tall, heavy, muscular, and broad-shouldered, but had had no training. So it was a competition between know-how and brute force. The city wrestler tried to use advanced tricks to overturn the muscled man, but with no success; however, the muscled man couldn't grab his opponent and throw him back-first on the mat. They struggled against each other for more than fifteen minutes without success. Ultimately, they were stopped and the match was declared a draw. From that event, I came to realize that brute force can, at times, outweigh technique.

There were many guys from Siberia in another platoon. After the morning run and exercises, they would pull a long hose out through the window in the washroom and spray their naked upper bodies, flushed and perspiring, in temperatures between 14°F and −4°F. Because I had never before seen

---

2   The army was concerned with soldiers' hygiene, but each soldier was only given two shirts per year. We could only wash them once a week (on weekends) and our morning routine included a hygiene check by our sergeant or by another officer. He would come along and examine our collars at morning inspection; if the collar looked greasy and dirty, there would be serious consequences. Hence, stitching the white cloth (which was made of old bedding) onto the collar nightly was a must.

such behavior, I took them for crazies. Eventually, I started to envy them and decided to try it for myself. Showering in such cold wasn't easy, but after a month of trying my body became accustomed to it, and by springtime I was able to shower when the temperature was way below freezing.

One guy from Siberia was Jewish, with the last name Friedman. He immediately recognized that I was a Jew and started approaching me by calling me a "dirty Jew." At first, I was very upset. Then I realized he was joking and answered him with the same words. He taught me how to protect myself from antisemitic insults. Antisemitism was mild in Siberia, and he hadn't suffered much from it, but after I told him how it had impacted our lives in Ukraine and Moscow, he was pretty sympathetic. We became friends and made a pact to help each other if needed.

Our training came to an end in April, and we were told that we would be sent to different air bases in the Soviet Union. One day, as I was working on the course material, Captain Kouchinsky entered the classroom, closed the door, showed me a list of airbases requesting new specialists, and asked me where I would like to go. I chose the base closest to Belgorod-Dnestrovsky, in a small town called Artziz, in Bessarabia. It was about a two-hour drive from my parents' home.

Two days later, Captain Kouchinsky informed me that I couldn't transfer to Artziz because the airbase had supersecret fighter jets (the Sukhoi Su-7). I was denied security clearance there because I was a Jew. But I was granted my second choice—an airbase a few miles from Sevastopol, Crimea. It was in a valley and near a hill called Belbeck, on the shore of the Black Sea. It was a beautiful and warm place.

Before our group departed for Sevastopol, I learned that Captain Kouchinsky had been promoted to the rank of major. I had wanted to ask him if he was a Jew, but somehow it didn't happen. He had treated me differently from the other soldiers in our class and he had allowed me to choose my next place to serve; he didn't, however, tell me why he was giving me such special treatment. Later in life, I figured out that the name Kouchinsky may well have been Jewish. Regardless, I remain grateful to him for helping me during my first six months in the army.

Airbase

In May 1965, our group of newly trained servicemen rode by train to Simferopol, Crimea. From there, we were taken by bus to our base in

Belbeck. There were more than 2,500 soldiers on the base, along with blocks of buildings for pilots, officers, and their families. There were few barracks for soldiers—one for the men who serviced fighter planes, another for those in the supporting services unit (such as those who worked on automobiles, helicopters, and so on). At the center of the base were the headquarters, medical unit, kitchen, and cantina. The base was encircled by a barbed wire fence more than six feet high—both to prevent illegal entry into the base and to stop soldiers from leaving without permission.

Beyond, there were peach orchards, vineyards, and a small river, the Belbeck, running into the Black Sea. On the other side of the Belbeck valley was another hill that was used as an artillery base. On top of the hill were giant cannons facing the Black Sea. Capable of shooting distances of twenty to twenty-five miles, they had been built just after World War II to protect Sevastopol's naval fleet from attacks from the sea. We were told that the ammunition was so heavy that special machinery was needed to load it. The machinery was deep underground; from our base, we could see only the guns. Once a year, the cannons were checked by shooting live ammunition into the sea. The villages in the Belbeck valley and the superiors at our base were notified a week ahead of time to prepare for this. We had to put masking tape on the windows to prevent them from cracking.

In our first year, we were labeled as green (*salagas*) and were given low-level tasks in addition to our regular duties. Once or twice a week, we were assigned work in the base's kitchen: cleaning the place, serving food three times a day, and washing dishes. It was arduous and dirty work. In addition, we were assigned responsibility for the security of the base, headquarters, and the runway on which the fighter jets were parked. Twice a month, I had to spend twenty-four hours as a member of a three-man team which was ordered to guard the base's headquarters with rifles loaded with live rounds. We all took watches: two hours as lookout, four hours rest. Security duty was also not easy—especially during the night. These extra duties were drastically reduced in my second and third years of service.

My platoon commander, Senior Lieutenant Yuri Mikhailov, was a young, intelligent, and cultivated guy who was still studying at the military academy. Every other week, the academy sent him a package of study materials for different subjects, along with problems to be solved. Once again, I got lucky: one of these subjects was math. When nobody was around, Yuri asked me if I could help him with his assignments. Of course, I agreed.

Reuven (far right) with friends in Sevastopol, summer 1965.

Once or twice a week, Yuri invited me to his apartment for a few hours to work on math. His beautiful young wife would prepare some homemade food, pour us each a glass of red wine, and then take part in our discussions about math and various other topics—but not politics. I enjoyed those occasions: I had a chance to go over some math topics that I had learned in my first year of university. I could find the things I had already forgotten in Yuri's books and then I would teach him what he would need for the military academy's exams, which he took twice a year.

When I visited Yuri's home, I also enjoyed the overall dining experience—china plates and real cutlery, as opposed to the crude and monotonous food provided in the soldiers' canteen. There, breakfast consisted of oatmeal, tea, and a small pat of margarine; for lunch we got soup, a small piece of pork, and a spoonful of buckwheat kasha (or barley, macaroni, or potatoes); and for supper we were given bread, some kasha, and tea. In the first year, I would often leave the dining hall feeling very hungry—particularly because I couldn't eat fatty pork. On the days when I was hungry after lunch, I would buy a can of kefir and a bun in the soldiers' shop.

Clothing was also limited, especially socks. In fact, we had no socks: we were only given square flannel cloth (*portiankas*) to wrap around our feet (two "pairs" each). Each week, when we showered—yes, only once a week—we used our second pair and washed the previous week's (we cleaned our own items by hand).

Slowly we settled into the routine: morning runs and exercises, breakfast, going to the runway (which was about two miles from our barracks) three or four days a week to work on fighter jets (regular maintenance of radio/radar equipment, repairing some things, or sending the electronic boxes to the lab for repair). We had to sit through political education classes a few times a week, which I found very boring and a stupid waste of time. In our free time in the evenings, we participated in sports activities, read newspapers and magazines, played billiards, and prepared for the next day.

My sergeant was in his third year of service. He was from Latvia, a place known for severe antisemitism. He couldn't mistreat me much because I was somehow looked after by our boss, Senior Lieutenant Yuri; instead, he frequently overscheduled my turns in the kitchen, guarding the runway, or protecting headquarters. When I tried to express my concerns, he looked at me with the emotionless eyes of a fish and repeatedly told me, "This is what it is."

While I was frustrated with the situation, I was bothered in the recreation room most of all. In our unit we had a large group of soldiers from the Uzbek Republic. They were Muslims and most were Jew-haters. Whenever I was playing billiards and more than two of them entered the room, they would push me away from the table, quietly saying, "Get out of here, dirty Jew." I tried to talk about it with my sergeant, but he advised me to just wait for them to finish their third year. However, one evening I couldn't take it anymore; I grabbed a billiard cue to beat them up. Fortunately for me, the other soldiers in the room grabbed me from behind, took the billiard cue from my hands, and walked me out. The Uzbek guys stayed at the table with sarcastic smiles. They had the upper hand: four guys, in their last year of service, with many other soldiers in my barracks who shared their antisemitic sentiments.

Many of the first-year soldiers who joined our unit were from small towns in western Ukraine. These young men, who generally were not well educated, had also had an antisemitic upbringing; however, they treated me reasonably well. I believe that they accepted me because I was somewhat sporty and had gone to university. They appreciated that I was able to show them exercises and gymnastics tricks (such as working on the parallel bars, vaulting, and exercising on the rings). They also had questions for me about attending university and living in Odesa. Because of their gratitude, these younger soldiers provided me with some physical protection from the Uzbeks and Latvians.

A few times every week, the pilots did special training flights. We had to go to the runway at least two hours before the scheduled flights to check our jets and ready them for takeoff. We knew every pilot personally; they all were friendly. These warm relationships made us work extra diligently, because we knew that any mistake on our part would jeopardize their lives.

An hour before the first flight, we would prepare a MiG 17—a two-seater jet with room for a pilot and navigator. It would fly to the zone where the exercises were being conducted to check conditions (wind, visibility, etc.). The regular flights would start once the MiG 17 crew reported that everything was favorable. Each pilot would fly three or four times each day. After each flight, we checked the electronic equipment; and once it was all in good condition, we would sign out until the next flight. Other groups looked at the hydraulics, fuselage, body, and engine of each jet. Others prepared and mounted armaments and refueled the planes. Each crew had to give the okay. The between-flight checks took up to thirty minutes to complete—which made flight days (or nights) very intense for us.

Sometimes we had sports competitions on our base (such as soccer and, during the summer months, swimming races in the Black Sea). I was one of the best in our unit at gymnastics, throwing javelins and grenades, swimming, volleyball, and goalkeeping in handball and soccer. Because of my athletic achievements, I was awarded a few unscheduled half-days off the base. I would take a bus, with a group of other soldiers, to Sevastopol, an important naval base on the Black Sea. We'd get off in the northern part of the city and take a twenty-minute ferry ride to the city center. Sevastopol was a lovely and clean southern city with lots of trees, small parks, and white buildings. We would walk aimlessly through the streets, explore its architecture, and watch people (primarily military and marine officers). When no officers were around, we would enter a gastronom to buy a half-liter bottle of vodka. And on the way back to our barracks, we would share it.

When we visited the city, the port was full of warships and submarines. Usually, as we wandered around Sevastopol, there were a lot of marine officers, and quite frequently we would meet a military patrol. According to military code, we were required to salute every officer and patrol we passed. When we encountered a patrol, we would be harassed because of our air force uniforms. We had to prove that we'd been allowed out of our base; then we were inspected to ensure that our boots and uniforms were in the proper condition. It was very embarrassing; however, we'd been forewarned of this eventuality, so we were prepared to behave appropriately. If we were troublesome, the patrols could either arrest us or send us back to our base to be punished by our commanders.

From time to time, something would occur on base to break the monotony of our lives. One morning, during inspection and the commander's announcements, the guard from a nearby peach orchard, armed with a rifle loaded with a good dose of salt, brought in four second-year soldiers who'd been caught picking fruit from the trees. Orchards in the Belbek valley grew large, tasty peaches with a rich, sweet fragrance. The soldiers had stashed their haul inside their green shirts—and they looked like pregnant girls! They stood before the commander with faces filled with guilt. "*Tovarishch* [comrade] colonel," said the guard, "I caught your boys in our orchard. Please punish them and order your soldiers to stop invading our orchards." The base commander thanked the guard and promised to improve our behavior. After the guard departed, the colonel ordered the four thieves to remove their shirts and spread the peaches out on the ground. While the rest of us laughed, the peaches were delivered to the kitchen, and all four soldiers received ten days imprisonment in the military prison in Sevastopol (there wasn't a prison on our base). The rest of us enjoyed the unexpected treat.

New Friends, New Responsibilities

In my second year of service, during a morning inspection, the colonel passed me and barked, "How come you have no stripes on your shoulder strap?" After I told him that I was *Private* Roman Rashkovsky, he became more upset and growled, "Tomorrow morning, you will have to have one stripe on your shoulder strap. You're lance corporal, and I will check that your shoulder strap reflects that." After the inspection, I asked my sergeant and Senior Lieutenant Yuri what I should do. There would be a disparity between my new rank and my army documents, in which I was identified as a private.

They told me not to worry, that they would take care of the situation. Thus, I received my first promotion.

That same year, a new group of soldiers arrived from training in Dniprodzerzhynsk. Among the newcomers were two Jewish guys, both of them from Moldova. One, Cogan (a typical Jewish surname), was married but hadn't yet had children. The other one, Alex, was a typical Jewish boy from a good family—full of life and a good sportsman. Though both men were assigned to the other wing, we quickly became friends. I didn't want them to experience the same humiliations at the hands of the antisemites on our base. In our free time we told one another our life stories, played sports, and shared the food we got in our parcels from home. Our solid friendship protected us.

I also got closer to another guy from the unit, Anatoly Glance, who was responsible for taking care of the jets' bodies and engines. At first, I wasn't sure if he was Jewish, because neither his first nor last names were particularly Jewish. Anatoly (called Tolik) had blood problems which caused a considerable amount of inflammation on his face and neck—once every few months he had to go to the hospital for a blood transfusion. Anatoly liked poetry, as did I, which helped us forge a bond that lasted throughout our time on base. He explained that his father, who was either Ukrainian or Russian, had left his family when Tolik was a little boy. So Tolik was raised by his mother and grandmother, who were Jewish. He took his mother's last name and considered himself a Jew and a Zionist. We were real buddies until he returned to Odesa after early demobilization due to his health. A few years later, I met him there, and our friendship continued through our civilian lives in the Soviet Union. But sometime in the summer of 1966, the evening before he was released from army service, we spent a particularly memorable time talking about life, literature, and other topics. Anatoly left me his copy of Isaak Babel's fabulous *Odessa Stories*. I still have it. On the day of his departure, I walked with him to the bus which would take him to the train station in Simferopol, the capital city of Crimea. While waiting for the bus, he pulled out a bottle of vodka and invited me to drink to his good fortune in his new life. We sat in the shadow of a tall tree and drank. It was sweltering, and the vodka was quite warm. I could only take a few gulps. Anatoly took the rest of it with him on his journey home.

Also that year, my Latvian sergeant finished his service and was replaced by a nice guy who had just started his third year. He was friendly and polite, and liked me. He seldom scheduled me for kitchen or guard duties; instead, he increased my technical responsibilities and invited me to begin mentoring younger soldiers. He also dreamed of getting more education after completing his mandatory army service. With him as my sergeant, my life stabilized and became more manageable. For good work, achievements in sports, and for being a good mentor to younger soldiers, I was awarded ten days' vacation to visit my family in Belgorod-Dnestrovsky in the fall of 1966.

The Secret American Spy Plane

As we approached spring, I was diagnosed with pneumonia. The medical unit at our base wasn't equipped to treat it, so I spent a few weeks at Sevastopol's central military medical facility. I went back to our base while it was still spring and was given a few days to rest, after which I was ordered to report to the runway to help with some work. I had to see a major, a KGB representative. When I got to the runway, I saw a strange scene. An Antonov military transport airplane, the largest plane in the world (much like the Lockheed C-130 Hercules), sat with its back gate open. On the grass beside the runway was a gigantic wing from an aircraft I'd never seen. The wing was much wider than the Antonov gate, so a group of soldiers with axes and other heavy tools were breaking it into pieces that could be loaded onto the transport. I was given a heavy hammer and a chisel to help out.

While we worked, other soldiers explained what was happening. It wasn't one of ours. The gigantic wing was from an American spy plane downed in the Black Sea by a rocket fired from a Soviet submarine. The aircraft had probably sunk, but this wing had broken off and stayed afloat. It had somehow been delivered to our base early that morning so that it could be taken to Moscow for further study. The wing was covered with a material that looked like honeycomb, about two inches thick (which, I assume, is what made the wing float). Coming into contact with an US plane—especially one that was engineered so differently from our own—felt magical. I couldn't believe what I was seeing.

The plane had been stationed in Turkey. Once or twice a week, when we changed the frequencies of our jets' radio and radar systems, an American aircraft would fly along the Soviet border in the Black Sea. It was equipped with an electronic laboratory that would listen in on, capture, or unscramble the frequencies of the radio, radar, and other systems in the Soviet Union's air force and navy. We would alter our radio frequencies at least once or twice a week and our plane identifier frequencies even more often. All our security systems were in a state of alert when the Americans were in flight; at least two Soviet pilots would sit in their jets, ready to intercept anything that came too close to the Soviet border. Sometimes our jets would fly parallel to the American aircraft to show our readiness to defend our borders. With our machines flying in a state-of-alert pattern, it took the Americans about an hour to figure out our radio and radar frequencies; after that, the plane would return to its base in Turkey. But that night it hadn't made it back.

About a week or two later, as I perused the army newspaper, I found a small article responding to a US complaint about the USSR's supposed downing of one of its craft. The article categorically denied any Soviet involvement or knowledge of the incident. That was the standard response by the authorities. But this time I knew the truth: after all, I had spent a half day loading wing pieces onto a transport plane! This blatant lie haunted me for years. If what the Americans were saying was true—and from my experience, I knew it was—then what were they doing so close to the Soviet border? My head was spinning with how much misinformation was out there—both beyond and within the Soviet Union.

At one point I was assigned to prepare a small MiG 17 to fly into a training zone to check meteorological conditions and survey the ground for potential threats and obstacles. An hour after takeoff, it returned to base having sent out an emergency landing signal. That was the first time in my almost two years of service that this had happened. We were all very stressed; we liked the pilot very much, and I had come to know his family well. It was still daylight as the plane was landing, and we saw antenna cable hanging from the jet's tail. It should have been stretched from the upper point of the tail to the back of the pilot cabin.

An announcement was made ordering Soldier X to report to the officer in charge of the day's training exercises. But he was nowhere to be found. We later learned that he'd gone to hide in the vineyards just outside of our base. He'd been responsible for the condition of the jet's body and engine. After fueling the plane before the flight, he hadn't closed the cap properly. It had flown off and sliced through the antenna. It was sheer luck that the pilot was able to navigate the jet back to our base. For his negligence, the next day Soldier X was sent to the military detention center in Sevastopol.

One day we had a traditional army menu with pasta and ground meat (*makarony po-flotski*). It was a change from buckwheat, barley, and oatmeal—and it was much tastier. But that day, many soldiers detected worms in their food and complained to the chef. He laughed and told them that it was additional protein. We were upset and took our plates to the medical unit, because the medical officer on duty had checked the food before allowing it to be served. He'd missed the worms. Like the chef, he said that the food was edible despite the worms and we should stop complaining. Somebody started yelling to remind him of the mutiny on a Russian battleship before the revolution (the subject of Sergei Eisenstein's famous 1925 movie *Battleship Potemkin*). The officer said nothing and disappeared inside the building. We could not do anything else: the military code didn't allow any deviation from commanders' orders; the result of such deviation would be imprisonment— or, in extreme cases, even execution.

Planning Ahead

Toward the end of my second year of military service, I started thinking about my return to civilian life. I realized that I had forgotten a lot of what I had learned during my first year of university, so I decided that, upon my return to Odesa, I would go back and retake my first-year courses. I also realized that my civilian passport was still the temporary (prison) one which I had been issued years before. I had my original birth certificate (in the name of Riven Rashkovsky) which I had spoiled with ink; but it was clear that I needed to resolve the issue of my personal documentation before I completed my stint in the army in the fall of 1967.

I wrote a letter to the registry department in the city of my birth, Uzbekistan, requesting a copy of my birth certificate. The new document arrived a few weeks later; it was summer 1966. Then, on one of my days off the base in the middle of the week, I went to Sevastopol and filed the necessary papers to change my first name from Riven to Roman. No explanations were needed and, in the fall of 1966, I officially became Roman Rashkovsky! They issued me a new birth certificate. With that, I could apply for a real passport and get it before going back home and starting university. I kept my old, temporary passport as a souvenir—but I had to destroy it before leaving the Soviet Union in 1971.

At one point, I realized that I was still dreaming about piloting a military jet. It had been my dream when I was very young—a dream that I had suppressed over time. However, working with planes and seeing pilots take off and land had rekindled my dream. I told Yuri, my lieutenant, about my desire to get into pilot school, and he promised to find out what I should do to apply. A few days later, he informed me that the maximum age for acceptance was twenty-one, which was exactly my age. To be admitted, he added, I would need to be in excellent health and to pass some academic exams. I was sure that I fulfilled all of the prerequisites and that I had quite a good chance of getting in.

I wrote the application, mailed it, and waited for my invitation to pilot school. More than a month passed with no reply. Then, one day while I was working on our jets on the runway, I heard an announcement ordering me to report to the head of the base's KGB representative at headquarters. As I stood in his office, he asked me if I had applied for admission to the pilot training program. I answered in the affirmative. The major pulled out my application from his desk and asked me why I wanted to be a pilot. I told him about my childhood dream and about the fact that I was at the maximum age to make such an application. I told him about my physical condition (that I was the base champion in many sports competitions) and about my standing as a university student in math. He listened to me and nodded his head.

Then he said that he wanted to ask me a question. He agreed with all I was saying; however, he said, there was one thing stopping me from realizing my dream. He asked me if I had relatives outside the Soviet Union. I suddenly understood the futility of my goal. Of course, he knew of my three aunts (my mother's sisters) living in Israel. After I confirmed my connections, the major lectured me on why I could never be a military—or civilian—pilot in the USSR.

The Soviet definition of nationality was strange and inconsistent. In most of the world, the concept of nationality entailed classifying people based on common ancestral land, language, and culture. That would be okay for Ukrainians, Uzbeks, and others—even if they lived in a different part of the USSR. After all, an Uzbek was an Uzbek, even if he lived in Moscow; a Ukrainian was a Ukrainian, even in Siberia. However, in the USSR, a Jew was a Jew if his father and mother were Jews. If at least one parent wasn't a Jew, then the child was given the opportunity to choose the nationality of the non-Jewish parent. Such was also the case for Germans who settled in Russia more than three hundred years ago. Soviet citizens were particularly concerned with their nationality status; it was a significant piece of information on their passports.

The major explained that even though I met all of the conditions for admission into the military's pilot training school, I would never be accepted because I had relatives who lived outside of the USSR (the fact that they lived in Israel was particularly problematic). I asked him if any Soviet Jew could be admitted. After thinking for a minute or two, he told me that it would be impossible. He said that there were more than a hundred nationalities in the USSR and that, if people from all the nationalities were allowed to be air force pilots, there was a risk that, should a pilot fly to the West and defect, the USSR could lose all of its planes. That was the end of it: on the one hand, the major confirmed that I would never be a pilot in the USSR; on the other, I took his words as an admission that most people in the USSR yearned to escape the communist paradise and that the KGB and the Soviet government were afraid of losing their air force.

Life as a *Starik*

In the fall of 1966, all third-year soldiers—we called them *stariki* (old men)— were demobilized from the army; by default, I became a starik, with all the unwritten privileges afforded them. Thus, during my third year of service, I had far fewer guard or kitchen duties than I'd had before. Instead, my primary responsibilities were to train young soldiers to service the jets and prepare them for flights. By that point, Yuri needed less of my help with his military academy studies; nonetheless, we continued being friends. I also developed a close relationship with another Jew, Yuri's counterpart in another unit, Senior Lieutenant Michael Golbin. Although he was much older than Yuri (about fifty), I liked to spend my free time visiting him in his lab.

I could openly discuss with Michael the difficulty of being a Jew in the Red Army. When I commented that it seemed strange that a man of his age had such a low military rank, he told me his life story. He had been drafted into the Red Army during the middle of World War II. Being better educated than most of the soldiers, he trained to service military planes. After the war, he completed officer's courses, was promoted to lieutenant, and continued to serve in the air force. However, he was promoted only once (to senior lieutenant), a few years after Stalin's death, and had stayed at this rank. He explained that he hadn't continued his education after World War II. Even without that extra education, he still could have been promoted to captain or major; however, given the rampant antisemitism in the USSR—a sentiment shared by his superiors—he had been routinely overlooked when it came time for promotions.

Certainly, he acknowledged, his low rank impacted his monthly salary and forced him to serve in the army well past the official retirement age of forty-five. And given that he wouldn't be able to find similar work outside of the army, he was loath to give up his free apartment in the officers' block. Michael often invited me to his place when his wife made a traditional Jewish supper. I felt at home with these lovely people.

Early in the spring of 1967, our wing was scheduled for training exercises in the Turkmenistan Desert east of the Caspian Sea. We loaded our tools and belongings into a transport plane and we were flown to the military base near Krasnovodsk (a four-hour flight from eastern Crimea, across the Black Sea, over the Caucasian Mountains, and across the Caspian Sea). The scenery was dramatically different from Crimea: the runway was surrounded on all sides by dunes of yellow sand; there were only a few barracks for soldiers; and there was one large dining facility. When we arrived in the canteen for supper, we found a few plates with garlic on each table—it was to compensate for the soldiers' lack of vitamins (there was a minimal supply of vegetables and fruits at the base).

When the jets arrived that first evening, we started our servicing routines. A few days later—after our pilots had undertaken several training flights in the desert and had practiced firing rockets from the MiG 19s—we were flown back to Sevastopol. We landed for a few hours at the base at the foot of the Caucasian Mountains on the way back. The fields around the runway were gorgeously green, the grass was tall, and the air was full of a springtime fragrance. I had never before experienced such drastic differences in scenery and climate.

Reuven with a MiG 19, 1966.

A week after returning to base, we had lots of work with our jets and stayed late at the runway. We were supplied with food from the kitchen and worked until dusk. That evening, our small unit of helicopters (four or five of them) was undertaking night training. While we ate with the pilots, I asked one of them what night training was like, and he jokingly invited us to take part in their flight (which would be about an hour and a half long). Yuri gave us the okay, and four of us took our places in the roomy belly of the helicopter. The objective of this flight was to get into a predefined zone, find an object on the ground, and bring it home—all in the darkness of a Crimean night.

It was my first time in a helicopter and it was a bit frightening: the flight was loud (from the engine outside the cabin), shaky, and bumpy; flares of fire came from the engine; and below us it was almost completely dark. As we entered the area where the search object was likely to be found we saw a small light on the ground. When the helicopter approached the site, we spotted a large pail with liquid in it. Without landing the craft, the pilot dropped a cable with a hook, captured the bucket, and brought it up. Then we flew back. We had a breathtaking view of Sevastopol at night as we passed around the city.

In May 1967, I was surprised by the delivery of a letter from my parents telling me that my mother had received a permit to visit her three sisters in Israel; she would travel there at the beginning of June and stay for two weeks. Mom would depart from Odesa on a liner bound for the Israeli port of Haifa (with stops en route in Istanbul and Cyprus). Of course, the permission was given only to my mother. Nobody from my family was allowed to accompany her. We were virtual hostages, held to make sure she returned to the wonderful Soviet Union. I was very excited for her—she'd dreamed about meeting her sisters since she'd tracked them down after Stalin's death. My mom had no relatives left in the Soviet Union; they had all perished during World War II at the hands of the Nazis and their Ukrainian henchmen.

Also in May, six months before my demobilization, I got word that I was to be promoted to sergeant. This would add about two extra rubles (which today would be roughly the equivalent of $5 USD) to my monthly military salary. It wasn't much—it would only allow me to buy a bottle of kefir and a bun ten days a month or buy ten packs of cigarettes—but it would still be some help. My promotion didn't mean a change in my responsibilities. I wouldn't, for example, be the commander of the four younger soldiers working with me, but I would continue to mentor them in their technical duties. I was pleased to avoid the added responsibility.

I only had a few months left of my army service and felt that I had finally attained some kind of peace with those around me. I feared that the promotion would draw attention to me and potentially create issues: perhaps it would provoke some antisemitism in those who hadn't been promoted; alternatively, it might disturb the hierarchy that was keeping me in a position where I was friendly with everyone and people let me be. I was known as the sportsman—and I didn't want to be the nail that stood up only to be hammered down. There weren't any advantages to accepting the rank, except, of course, the meager two rubles per month.

If I refused the promotion, I would be sent to a military prison—which, I thought, would be manageable. I'd been told that, most of the time, detainees were required to practice marching, clean floors, and do other moderately unenviable tasks. It seemed best to keep things as they were, even if it meant some minor grief at the base. I discussed my situation with Yuri, but he insisted that I be promoted to recognize my quality service. He also told me that the application had already been submitted so it would take a few weeks to announce my new rank. I was upset about the inevitability of everything and started thinking about how to avoid it.

Finally, I came up with a plan: I would become visibly drunk to the point that my superiors would notice. My punishment for drinking on the base could range from my denial of the promotion (the easiest—and wanted—outcome) to a sentence of fifteen days of incarceration in military prison (the maximum punishment—which, frankly, didn't seem that bad). Regardless of the consequences, this was my way out. But I had no way to purchase alcohol on the base. Also, a vodka bottle cost around three rubles (almost my monthly pay as a soldier).

However, alcohol could be obtained, albeit not entirely legally. Each MiG 19 jet had a three-liter container filled with medical alcohol (about 96 percent proof) which was used to prevent the accumulation of water or ice on the jet's window as it flew through clouds. It was well known that soldiers servicing jets stole some of this alcohol. Sometimes I was awakened at two or three in the morning and invited to drink in the small storage room.

It is very dangerous to consume 96 percent alcohol, but there is a way. The stariki introduced the younger ones to the method: (a) pour fifty milliliters of the stuff into a drinking cup; (b) put the blade of a knife into the cup, making sure it is touching the bottom; (c) take tomato juice and pour it very slowly on top of the blade (if it is done slowly enough, the tomato juice will settle at the bottom of the glass without mixing with the alcohol);

(d) stop pouring when the cup seems to be about half alcohol and half juice; (e) prepare something small to eat (we had bread for that); (f) gulp a second glass of warm water (to wet the throat); (g) immediately start drinking alcohol/tomato juice (drink fast and continue drinking until you reach the bottom: there can be no interval between drinking the alcohol and drinking the tomato juice); and (h) eat a piece of bread and be proud of yourself. After our almost-nightly sessions, we'd go back to our beds to have another few hours' sleep. Honestly, I didn't like this regular consumption of alcohol—I didn't even like vodka—but I couldn't refuse to participate lest my friends fear that I was reporting on them.

June 4 was a Sunday and no activities were scheduled for our jets. The soldiers had a day off to take care of their laundry, play sports, write letters, watch TV, and so on. To prevent my promotion, I cooked up a scheme with four guys who had to be on duty at the runway. I promised these guys that I'd cook them a fish soup, on the condition that they get some fresh fish from the sea. One of our officers used to put nets to catch fish in the sea just below one end of the runway. By the time I arrived, my friends had a few large mackerel and some smaller fish. When I cleaned up the catch and started cooking, my friends procured half a liter of alcohol from a few jets. They already had some bread and vegetables for the party. I'd learned the recipe for fish soup when my mom worked at the fish factory. It was simple to make, and it came out very tasty.

We started our supper at about five o'clock. No officers or other soldiers were around. We sat, ate, and drank our medical-grade booze. The drink hit me quickly; indeed, my memory of that evening is fuzzy. We joked, ate, and drank into the night. I remember that there was a flash—a powerful searchlight was illuminating the runway. It swept to the vineyards surrounding the runway and then pointed at Sevastopol, a few miles away. I went down to the barracks—not by the regular road, but by the narrow trail through the bushes down the hill. I fell a few times, but managed to make it back to headquarters. I remember standing in front of an officer on duty and lecturing him about being a good human being. The next thing I remember is lying on my bed fully clothed the following morning; everyone around me was rushing to get ready for morning inspection and announcements. I joined the crowd and asked a few guys what had happened the night before, but nobody wanted to tell me how I got into the barracks and onto my bed.

It was early morning, June 5, 1967. Everyone was lined up in the central square. The officers inspected us, the base commander gave a short speech and made some announcements. At the end, he called my name. I took three steps forward and listened to what he had to say. He said that the day before I had behaved despicably, in a way unbecoming of Soviet soldiers, by consuming alcohol and disturbing my surroundings. I was to be incarcerated in the Sevastopol military prison for fifteen days. He sent me to work in the kitchen until my transport came, which was scheduled for later that afternoon. Work in the kitchen was humiliating for a starik; but for me it was okay because my sentence ended my promotion.

I started working in the kitchen immediately. First, I helped with putting breakfast on the tables and, after the soldiers had eaten, I collected the dirty aluminum plates and spoons for washing. There were about ten younger soldiers working with me. The soldiers at the base couldn't all eat together because the dining hall wasn't large enough; thus, every meal had to be served twice.

The Six Day War

As I was finishing washing the dishes, a loud siren suddenly went off. It was very unusual because sirens would only be sounded during special training events, and we would know about them at least a week before. I continued my work, but after ten or fifteen minutes I realized that I was alone in the kitchen. I ran outside, but there was no one in sight. I put on my shirt and ran to headquarters. The first officer I met there told me that war had broken out in the Middle East between Israel and a group of Arab countries (what would become known as the Six Day War). The whole base was now in alert mode: everyone was on the runway and our jets were ready for flight.

My first thought was about my unit and the pilots. I was worried about new young soldiers servicing the MiG 19s. I believed that they were negligent; there had been a few times when they'd left tools on the ground underneath the jets' engines. Without thinking twice, then, I ran to where my unit should have been. Yuri said that it was nice I'd joined them instead of waiting in the kitchen for my prison sentence—and he meant it. He was happy to see me alongside those in my unit. All our jets were lined up along the runway, and the pilots were sitting inside. We checked the condition of our radio and radar equipment while the other specialists went over the hydraulics, engines, and other jet parts. I asked Yuri about what was going on in the Middle East, but he didn't know much. Pilots rotated in shifts; they would sit in the jets for an hour, and then another group of pilots would replace them for an hour. This went on for the whole day. We were at high alert. At night we slept on the ground beside the planes.

In the morning the alert level was reduced, and only four of our jets had pilots sitting in them in anticipation of an order to fly. I went to Michael Golbin's unit to see what was going on in the Middle East. Uncle Misha (as I had come to call him) said that he'd listened to the radio and that the news had reported the following: Egypt had attacked Israel from the south and would soon be in Be'er Sheva, the largest city in the Negev; Syria had attacked from the north and heavily bombarded the port city of Haifa; Syrian tanks were rolling down from the Golan Heights toward the Mediterranean Sea; and finally, Jordan had attacked central Israel, bombing the cities of Tel Aviv and Petah Tikva, leaving them to burn. I was in shock. My mom was visiting her sisters in Petah Tikva. Uncle Misha knew this, and he tried to calm me down. He said that Moscow was delivering news based on information coming from Arab sources. He asked me to try not to worry too much and wait until there was more information. Despite his assurances, I was worried sick and remained so over the next few days.

Reuven's aunt Rivka, his mother Lea, and his aunt Zipora in Israel, 1967.

Nobody came to take me to prison, and Yuri told me to lie low and not say anything; he needed me to help with our work. Then, on the fourth or fifth day of the alert, we were told that a colonel from army headquarters in Kyiv had arrived to update the staff on the situation. Hundreds of us, including officers and pilots, gathered beside the runway to hear the latest news.

The colonel informed us that the Arabs had lost their entire air force on the morning of the first day of the war (June 5). The Soviet army strategists had learned some important lessons. First and foremost, he said, we needed to move all our jets to random positions around the runway (the Egyptian jets had parked on their runway in one line while their pilots had their breakfast; the Israelis had easily and swiftly destroyed them). The colonel also told us that, in the near future, we would have to construct underground garages for our aircraft—again, in random places. He told us that the Arab soldiers had received low-quality training, or perhaps the disaster was because they prayed five times a day; even during a battle they left the battlefield and removed their boots to pray. Perhaps their officers were lying in their reports to their superiors. All in all, the colonel gave us a very grave picture of events. Finally, he informed us that we were expecting the arrival of a lot of jets from various Soviet bases—as well as jets from Poland, Romania, and other countries in the Eastern Bloc. These planes were going to fly to Syria and Egypt to replenish lost equipment. The Soviet Union was determined to help its Arab allies fight against the imperialist and capitalist Zionist aggressors.

The evening after this presentation, I walked into Uncle Misha's office to talk about what we'd heard. His speech had inspired a great deal of excitement in me—and happiness; bad news for the Arabs meant safety for my family. Of course, I'd hidden my relief from the soldiers and officers. Uncle Misha and I spoke very quietly so that we wouldn't be overheard. He smiled and told me that I shouldn't worry about my mom; it was quiet in Israel and, he assured me, the war was almost over.

The next day, more than a hundred jets from all over the Soviet Union and the Eastern Bloc landed. At night, we were told to be ready to work on these planes. But this was a different kind of work. First, each soldier got a zinc pail full of a liquid with which to remove Soviet and Eastern Bloc identifiers from the jets slated for Syria and Egypt. This took me by surprise. I started panicking at the thought of supplying jets to Israel's enemies while my mom was there. My first reaction was to refuse the order, but after some thought I decided to consult Uncle Misha.

When I told him what was going on, he sat me down and spoke quietly about the implications of refusing to act on orders from superior officers. We were still on high alert (which is equivalent to being at war). According to the army code, disobedience would result in at least twenty-five years of imprisonment in a labor camp in Siberia or a death sentence.

Uncle Misha asked me to consider my predicament. More than two thousand soldiers were serving on the base, so the work would be done with or without me. But if I refused, what would happen to me, my mom, and my family? Was the punishment worth it just to make a point? What good would come of it? He advised me to put my head down and do as I was told. Uncle Misha had brought me to my senses. I returned to my unit, and we worked all night removing the insignia and sending the planes south in the dark of night. During WW2, Stalin had said, "It takes a brave man to be a coward in the Red Army;" as I worked I couldn't shake off unsettling thoughts about what would inevitably happen to a brave but insubordinate man in the Red Army!

The following day, giant transport aircraft landed; they brought a few hundred soldiers dressed in the black uniforms of marine paratroopers. They rested on the grass beside the runway across our unit, but we were not allowed to approach them or to talk with them. They were flown away from the base that evening. We learned that their destination was Lebanon, but the information was a secret. Most of the transport planes returned about ten or fifteen days later. After they left, rumors (which were more than plausible) spread that those who hadn't returned had been lost with a platoon (or perhaps two) during some action in Lebanon.

Leaving the Army

A few weeks after the end of the Six Day War, the alert level was reduced and eventually brought back down to low. We returned to our regular routines, and my fifteen-day prison sentence appeared to have been forgotten. I was forgiven, I guess, because of my dedication to our unit and the work I had done. I asked Yuri if I should still expect some punishment, but he told me to keep quiet about it.

As autumn approached, I received a letter from home telling me that my mom had finally got back from Israel. Although she'd had a traveling visa and permit from the Soviet authorities for two weeks, she had been trapped because of the Six Day War. And because the embassy was closed, she prolonged her stay as long as possible, finally returning in September. I was very much relieved.

During my last two months in the army, I waited impatiently for a call from headquarters that would mean the end of my service and my return to civilian life. Most of my fellow stariki started getting sent home at the end of September, but I didn't until mid-October. I was working on the jets when I got a call to report to headquarters in thirty minutes. The officer on duty there informed me that I would go home soon, and then he started my release procedure. He gave me a list of the approvals I would need for my release: first from the medical unit, then from the barracks foreman, and finally from the human resource officer. Getting them wasn't difficult, but it still took about two days. After that, I met Yuri and his wife at their place to say goodbye and thank them for all of the support they'd given me during my time in the army. I also met with Uncle Misha and his wife to thank them for treating me like their son and saving me from getting into serious trouble during the Six Day War.

My last meeting was with the human resource officer. He gave me a bag containing the things that I'd surrendered at the Military Aviation Mechanical School in Dniprodzerzhynsk three years earlier—my civilian clothes, shoes, and a few other belongings. He got upset when he found my passport was missing. I told him not to worry as it was waiting for me at home. I was ready and eager to leave the base, but I had to wait until the next morning. I was allowed to go off-site for two hours; I used this opportunity to walk to the village nearby to get a bottle of vodka and some food. That evening, I met with my Jewish friends to celebrate my return to civilian life. We found a secluded place beside the sports facilities to drink and eat. I gave them my last tips on surviving on the base and avoiding unnecessary conflicts by sticking together.

CHAPTER 4

Back to University

_____

Settling In

The following morning, I picked up my belongings and papers from HQ and started my journey back to real life. When I was through the base's gate, I made a vow not to return to Crimea for at least ten years and to not eat buckwheat for twenty years!

I arrived in Odesa by train in mid-October. I first needed to reinstate myself as a student—which, knowing how bureaucracy works, I anticipated would take at least two days. In full military uniform, I walked through the entrance of the building and up to the administrative office of the Math Faculty, where I explained that I had been drafted into the army three years ago and would like to get back to my studies. The receptionist pulled out a notebook from her desk, found my name, and went to another room to retrieve my file. When she came back, I asked her if I could go back to the first year of math classes, to which she said that there were instructions from the top that every returning soldier was required to return to the program from where he had left in 1964. I had only two choices: go start in the second year or drop out. I chose the first option. It took me another day to settle into the dormitory and prepare for university.

I then took a train from Odesa—still in full uniform—to Belgorod-Dnestrovsky to spend a weekend with my family. My parents were already home from work when I arrived. There were tears of happiness as I stood surrounded by my parents, sister Emma, and brothers Fima and Izia. Hanna was working as a teacher in a village far from home. After supper, I was eager to hear from my mother about her visit to Israel.

It was thanks to the International Red Cross that she'd managed to go to Israel at all. The Red Cross, which was keen on reconnecting families that had been torn apart during the Second World War, had helped her establish contact with her sisters. In the years of the slight thaw that followed Khrushchev's accession to power and denunciation of Stalin, it was possible to apply directly to the authorities to visit or reconnect with family abroad. My mother had been granted permission. Her sisters had left in the late 1920s, when my mother was quite young, and emigrated to become pioneers in Palestine as single young women. It was unclear to me why they'd left Bessarabia, but I suspected it was poverty, antisemitism, and so they could pursue a dream.

My mom told us about our family in Israel—her three sisters and many of my cousins—and about the life she'd seen there. When I asked her about the Six Day War, she laughed and said that it was strangely peaceful inside Israel throughout. Most of the Israeli soldiers and reservists were located on three fronts: in the Sinai Desert, the Golan Heights, and in the east facing Jordan. Despite the war, my mom had enjoyed her time, bonding with her sisters and their kids. She showed me many photos.

I told her about the red alert on our base and how I'd helped send MiG 19 and MiG 17 jets to Syria and Egypt. I told her about the life-saving advice Uncle Misha gave. My mother mentioned that she'd been called to the local KGB offices a few times to explain why she hadn't returned home immediately after the Six Day War started. They wanted information about what she saw there during the war and where my cousins served in the Israeli Defense Forces.

Her explanation was that the embassy shut when the Soviet Union broke diplomatic ties with Israel. And, of course, my mom didn't see or hear any military secrets. The KGB interrogators pressed hard to make my mom reveal something valuable to them, but she'd only seen her family. Eventually, the KGB came down hard on her: she was demoted at the fish factory, her salary was cut by one-third, and she was still being harassed almost weekly.

My little brother Izia, ten years younger than me, studied violin at the city's musical school. My father was proud that at least one of his children would become a violinist. Our father had ensured that Izia would make something of his musical aptitude: if the boy didn't want to play, Dad would lock him in our parents' bedroom until he had perfected his playing. It was tough love, but it certainly set Izia on a course for success.

Finally in civilian clothing (mainly stylish, good-quality clothes brought from Israel by my mom) I took a train back to Odesa to resume my second year of studies at the university. The dormitory I was sent to for the 1967–68 school year was about one hundred yards from the building which housed the math and physics faculties. I shared a room with four other students; they had all been my classmates three years earlier and they were now in their final year. We bonded again; they had been in my situation, having returned from the army in 1963. The following morning a new student, just demobilized, came to our room. Aleksandr (Sasha) Svirski had served three years in East Germany and was starting his second year of studies at the Math Faculty. We all walked together to the university building for our first lecture.

Catching Up

Most of the one hundred and fifty students in the auditorium were new to me and about three years younger. Given that they had already spent about a year and a half together, they knew one another well. It was a strange feeling being a stranger in the classroom, and it took me more than a month to settle in. It was also hard to follow the professors' lectures and sift through unfamiliar material, old and new. We had only two months until the end of the semester and winter exams. I badly needed to get back up to speed with first-year calculus, higher algebra, and other topics. I realized that the only way to be ready for the December exams was to dedicate all my time to start from the beginning and, at the same time, learn the new material. As I talked about it with Sasha, he admitted that he was in the same predicament and was as scared as I was that he wouldn't pass the exams. We made a deal: every day after eating lunch, we would go back to the math building, find an empty room with a blackboard, and work hard on catching up with the previous year's material while studying the new material. We vowed to stay away from student parties, abstain from alcohol, and certainly not date girls. We dedicated our time and effort to our survival.

Sasha and I would barricade our room's door. The Math Faculty used three heavy classic calculus books by Professor Grigorii Fikhtengol'ts, one volume for each school year. Sasha and I would take turns proving theorems and solving problems from Fikhtengol'ts on the blackboard. It took us about two weeks to catch up on calculus. Suddenly I had an accurate understanding of fundamental mathematical concepts and methods of problem-solving in calculus. Every day of the week, we worked from about three to eleven in the evening—except for the few weekends when we visited our families, mine in Belgorod-Dnestrovsky and Sasha's in Pervomaisk (about thirty-five miles from Odesa).

One Friday in November, as we returned to the dormitory, the guys in our room invited us to the dormitory's party room for a dance with students from the faculties of language, literature, and philosophy. Sasha and I first refused: we were tired after spending so many hours in a closed room plowing through the hard math material; ultimately, however, we gave up and joined the party. Sasha, tall and handsome, was mobbed by the girls straightaway, and he spent the evening dancing with them. I approached a nice-looking girl standing alone by the window—Maria. We started talking; she told me that she was a first-year student in the Language and Literature Faculty. She was very worried about the upcoming winter exams because she was unable to get through the heavy load of reading. As we danced, she confessed that, being from a small town, she hadn't got to know the ancient Greek myths and stories that she needed for her exams—and now she had fallen behind. I told her about my fascination with this literature when I was in junior high school, and I promised to explain it to her and pass on my knowledge. But it had to be in the evenings after I'd finished studying math.

So we made a deal: Maria would meet me in the party room every evening with her books for the next few weeks. I would give her a summary of the important stories and tell her my views on their meanings, how they reflected the life of ancient Greece, the religion of Greece at the time, history, science, philosophy, and more. I was surprised at how much I remembered from fourth, fifth, and sixth grades and how my mind organized all of the material into a big picture. After a while, we started going out at night to get some fresh air, and slowly this turned into hugs and kisses. But it stopped abruptly one evening. We were walking at night on Pushkin Street, one of the nicest streets in Odesa, with old chestnut trees by the sidewalks and Italian and French-style buildings. It was tranquil at night, but as we approached the Philharmonic building some sparrows settling for the night on a chestnut tree made a loud noise. Maria started laughing and said that if she had a rifle, she would shoot the *zhids* from the tree.

I felt a sensation akin to a rash spreading across my body. *Zhid* (dirty Jew in Russian) is a word used by antisemites to humiliate Jews. Maria probably didn't know that I was Jewish—nor, perhaps, the meaning of the word. However, I suddenly felt a massive wall between us, and I lost interest in her. I stopped helping her and I avoided her. A few times the guys from my room told me that Maria had come looking for me and asked them to tell me that she was worried about me. I asked my friends to tell her that I was too busy with my studies and wasn't available anymore. After the winter exams, we ran into each other; she thanked me for all the help I'd given her and told me that she'd got 80 percent on her exam on the literature of ancient Greece. She asked me why I suddenly disappeared, but I couldn't tell her the real reason. I said that I had no time for anything except my studies.

Sasha and I worked very hard for the exams in December. As a result, I gained more confidence in my ability to understand the higher math material. We had five exams in December, and my marks were markedly higher than in my first year of study: I got 80 percent in four subjects and 60 percent in one. Our labors paid off! But, most importantly, I began to understand the beauty of calculus and started seeing a natural, logical progression of theoretical material in calculus, algebra, and other subjects. Learning became enjoyable and more effortless. The second session ended in mid-June 1968; this time I got 95 percent in three subjects and 85 percent in two. Sasha also finished this year with excellent marks, and we committed ourselves to continuing our mutually beneficial cooperation in our studies in the next school year.

Summer Break

In the summer of 1968, I went home to spend time with my family. I needed money to buy shoes and some dressy clothing—and I neither could nor wanted to ask my parents to help me out. They both worked a lot to provide for my sisters and brothers, and because of her adventure in Israel the summer before, Mom's salary had been cut and we still lived in poverty. With my neighbor and friend, Vitaly Ivanov, I obtained temporary summer work at a wine factory, where our job was to clear and organize the junk which filled a massive basement warehouse.

I liked spending my weekends at beaches on the Black Sea. The Dniester River enters the sea about twelve miles from Belgorod-Dnestrovsky. On the southern bank is Bugaz, a long-established, much-visited place for summer vacationers; on the northern side is Karolino-Bugaz (meaning Kings on Bugaz), which had been under redevelopment for about ten years. There were a few sanatoriums there that belonged to various companies from cities in the Soviet Union. My sister Emma was studying in the culinary profession at that time, and she worked during that summer in a sanatorium belonging to a Moscow firm. She provided me with accommodation for the weekends and, to justify my being on the premises, she told her supervisor that I was assisting her in the kitchen. To prove it, she asked me to help her remove meat from cow and pig carcasses. These tasks required careful work with sharp knives and knowledge of how to remove bones from half a cow or half a pig. I had these skills after working a summer at the slaughterhouse. I worked half a day in the kitchen and enjoyed suntanning on the beach and swimming in the sea after work.

One day on the beach, I met a Jewish family from Moscow: a couple and their young son, Jacob, who was about ten years old. They were playing the card game preference, a Russian version of bridge. I introduced myself and asked if it would be okay to join them for a game. As the four of us were playing, I noticed how smart their son was, and I tested his math and logical thinking. His parents invited me to join them again whenever I was there.

One day, while I was showing Jacob my gymnastic and acrobatic skills, a girl passing by on the beach demonstrated to us her gymnastics abilities. She was tall, in ninth or tenth grade, older than Jacob. She was staying with her parents in another sanatorium. She asked if she could meet with us so we could spend time together. We became friends and turned our friendship into a game. We played cards and did some gymnastics and acrobatics on the sand. Somehow, Jacob became Agent 1, I became Agent 2, and Nina, the new member of our team, became Agent 3. It was a strange friendship between two kids and me, completely innocent and built on intellectual abilities and a sense of humor. I didn't know then that my ability to establish rapport with kids and engage them intellectually would later be the foundation of an important part of my life.

Reuven with his young friend Jacob, "Agent #1," on the Black Sea shore, 1969.

The work Vitaly and I were doing at the wine factory was going well. We completed a big chunk of it by the end of the first week of August. We tidied up the area around the warehouse and reported our progress to the manager.

He was very impressed and admitted that he didn't expect us to finish the task that summer. He wrote a note to the company's accountant to pay us for what we'd already accomplished. For me, it was a handsome sum—enough to purchase things I needed for the next school year. I tried to give the remaining money to my mom, but she didn't want to take it; she said that I would need the money in Odesa.

Moving to Israel?

One evening, my parents asked to speak with me. They informed me that they had decided that our family should emigrate to Israel and that they needed my help. There were two reasons for their desire to move: first, my mother was eager to join her sisters (especially after her visit, which had left her with a wonderful impression of life there); and, second, there were rumors going around that "now was the time" to put pressure on the Soviet government to release those who wanted to emigrate.

My initial reaction was disbelief that the Soviet government would ever allow us out of the country. I had heard that the government persecuted Jews who petitioned by kicking them out of their workplaces or, at best, demoting them and denouncing them as traitors and agents of Zionist imperialism at public town hall-type meetings. Within such families hoping to emigrate, any students were kicked out of university and couldn't find jobs where they lived. The inability to work or study created a self-perpetuating myth: these Zionists were clearly parasites and, after six months of officially being unemployed, they could be deported to a village up to thirty-five miles away from their city in which they lived and forced to work on a collective farm.

My parents were aware of these abuses by the government, but they were determined to try to use the notion of family reunification to leave the Soviet Union. They asked me to write a letter to my mom's sisters requesting an invitation to the family to join them in Israel. With such a letter, we could start our bid to leave the USSR. I wrote to my aunts and let my parents wait for a response.

I returned to Odesa one week before the start of the new school year. I needed some time to find a place in the dormitory, get textbooks and other books from the university library, and take care of a few other formalities. I was sent to another dormitory, five blocks from the faculty. This dormitory was for students doing math, physics, or chemistry. The building was old and there was a strong stink of chlorine from the shared washroom on the first floor. On the second floor was a small party room with a television, a few tables, and some chairs. At the entrance hall in the dormitory was a security desk occupied by a superintendent and her subordinate, whose jobs were to prevent unauthorized persons from entering the premises.

To receive a bed in the dormitory, we had to pass sanitary and epidemiology checkups at an assigned clinic. To get books from the library, I had to obtain a reading list from the faculty's office. I then had to bring a stack of twelve to fourteen books to the dormitory and store them in the suitcase under my bed. (We didn't have to pay for our textbooks, but we were required to return them to the library at the end of the year before summer vacation.)

Back to School

I started my third year of university on September 1, 1968. Again, Sasha and I dedicated ourselves to our studies. Every afternoon we spent many hours in the university's study rooms going through new material, proving theorems, and solving problems. I was very excited about differential geometry and put hours into problem-solving work in my tutorial class.

However, I still ran into trouble during the exam. As I entered the exam room, three students were already preparing to present their work to Professor Siniukov. I picked up my assignment, which included a few questions on theory and a few exercises. As I took my place at the table behind one of the students, a few of them passed me a paper with questions for me to solve for them. Feeling confident in my skills and trying to be a supportive friend, I solved their problems and gave them back while Professor Siniukov was not looking at us. As the students whom I helped demonstrated "their" work to the professor, I finished my own exam preparations. The three students I helped got excellent marks using my solutions.

When it was my turn, I sat down at the professor's desk and showed him my work. He looked at it and asked me why I used notation precisely like those of the previous three students. I didn't want to expose my friends, so my response was that I didn't know. However, I said I knew the material well and was good at problem-solving. As I demonstrated my knowledge, the professor stopped me and said he couldn't give me a mark higher than 3 (60 percent). I was upset and asked him to examine me thoroughly to prove my knowledge of the material. He said that it was unnecessary, and he asked me to give him my exam book record to record the score. I looked into the professor's eyes and saw the same expression as in the eyes of the professor at Moscow State University during my entrance exams there—the icy, contemptuous look of the antisemite. I realized that there was no point in arguing. I got my 60 percent mark.

When I walked out of the room, the three guys I helped with their exams thanked me profusely, visibly upset about my mark. As I was standing there, disoriented and troubled, our teaching assistant told me that he was shocked by my low score. He said that that he'd given Professor Siniukov a list of the best students who attended his practicum before the exams, and I was at the top of the list. I told the TA the truth about what had happened, without giving away the names of the students I'd helped. The TA informed me that I could apply to the university appellation committee for a reexamination to improve my mark. If I did so, he would oversee my reexamination.

I did as he suggested and, at the end of the next week, my mark changed from 3 to 5 (excellent). I felt a mixture of relief and distress—we all knew I had the knowledge to deserve the 5 and I didn't feel that I should have had to jump through these hoops. As for the help I gave my friends, it wasn't exactly cheating: the culture of the Soviet Union in those days was such that everyone knew that many aspects—if not all—of the system we lived under were false. Helping friends was the right thing to do. I sailed through my winter exams with high marks, but the scar inflicted by Professor Siniukov caused me pain for a long time.

In the second semester, we were streamed into different specialist study groups and we had to work on a third-year thesis. I participated in a seminar given by Professor Vladimir Kostin on the stability of periodic differential equations that revolved around a theory written by the mathematician Nikolai Erugin. In short, Erugin proved that systems of differential equations with periodic coefficients could be transformed into systems with constant coefficients, but he hadn't provided methods for doing so. In other words, it was a nice theory but not practical. During one of the seminars, I asked if the theory could be extended to perturbed periodic systems and, if so, how to find perturbation limits. After the seminar Professor Kostin told me that my question was interesting, and that he would like to offer me this subject for my third-year thesis. If my work resulted in visibly good results, we could extend the inquiry into my master's thesis and, probably, into a doctoral study. I agreed and decided to join a group working on systems of differential equations under his supervision.

Reuven (top far left) with his classmates in the differential equations group, University of Odesa, 1968.

One of the students in this group, Galina Kirova, was employed part time in the faculty office. She approached me one day and invited me to her home for supper with her mother and grandmother. They lived in a lovely building not far from Odesa's beautiful Opera House, built by Italian and French architects. The three generations of women occupied one large room. Galina's mother, who was divorced, was a mezzo-soprano at the Odesa Philharmonic Theater. Her old, half-deaf, and sick grandmother occupied a corner behind a large armoire. During supper, Galina's mother said that she had heard lots of good things about me and that she wanted to ask me a favor: to help Galina with her year-end thesis. In return, she promised to provide me with tickets to concerts at the Philharmonic Theater. I asked Galina the nature of her thesis and figured out that I could help without compromising my own studies. So, for the last half year, I worked on her thesis and my own.

On one of my visits to my family in Belgorod-Dnestrovsky, my parents informed me that they'd received an official letter—an invitation to immigrate to Israel from my mom's sisters. It was a bit of a shock; I hadn't expected such a quick response from Israel. And I wasn't ready to commit myself to leaving the Soviet Union before graduating from university. I shared my doubts with my parents, but they insisted that we must get out of the country. After I saw that my parents were taking a firm stand on this, I agreed to help them with the paperwork requested by the OVIR (the department of the Soviet police that issues exit visas). I was still hoping that it would take a long time for them to get permission to move. I had heard lots of scary stories about what happened to people who applied for these visas: persecution at work and university; the inability to find a job; removal from the cities they lived in; and in some cases, even imprisonment. Toward spring, my parents received all the necessary forms from OVIR, and I diligently filled them in. A month after they'd applied for the visa, the OVIR asked for reference letters from their places of work and their children's educational institutions.

I had no choice but to obtain a reference letter from the university. I knew that the moment I made the request, I would be condemned for treason and vilified both for my desire to move to Israel and for being a Zionist. Then they would expel me. I tried to find a way out—and a brilliant idea crossed my mind. I approached Galina and told her that, in the coming summer, I might be able to travel as a tourist to one of the countries in the Soviet Bloc, but that I hadn't decided where to go. I added that I needed a letter from the university saying that I was a loyal citizen, a good student, and that the university was okay with my traveling abroad. I asked her to type me such a letter and leave a blank space for the country I would be visiting. Since I was working on Galina's thesis, she agreed; she typed the letter and used the university's stamp.

My next step was to find somebody with a typewriter similar to the one used in the faculty office. It wasn't easy, but the opportunity came surprisingly quickly. In the wintertime, my mother told me about a man in Odesa who had traveled on the same boat with her to and from Israel. He had told her that his son-in-law had a PhD from Moscow University and was now working in Odesa. He gave my mom his address and said that, if our family decided to go to Israel, his son-in-law was willing to help us emigrate. My mom passed the man's address on to me, and one day I went to his place.

The man (with his wife, daughter, and son-in-law) lived not too far from my dormitory. I introduced myself and spent a pleasant evening with the family. Michael (Misha) Sonis showed me his PhD thesis in functional analysis and algebra. I didn't understand his work, but it seemed impressive, and I later realized that it really was.

Misha worked at the Odesa Academy of Agriculture as a mathematician, and he invited me to seminars organized by Professor Mark Krein from the Technical University of Construction. Professor Krein was a member of the Academy of Sciences of Ukraine, a well-known mathematician home and abroad. His seminars focused on the stability of differential equations in Banach spaces, an area very close to my field of study. He had many achievements in math and had gained international fame and status. Despite this, he wasn't allowed to work at our university because of his controversial past: in the fifties, he'd been kicked out because he was a religious Jew who wore a kippah. So he'd had to settle for lowly work as head of the Math Department at the Technical University of Construction, a second-class school.

Krein's seminars were attended by his PhD students—mostly Armenians and Jews—and Jewish math professors from various institutions in Odesa (such as those specializing in agriculture, cooling technology, shipbuilding, communications, etc.). This enthusiastic group of people enjoyed complexity and were united by their love of math. They had lively discussions that were way beyond my understanding. The leaders of the seminar were a husband and wife, the Rotermans, and they led the review of the content of a manuscript written by Mark Krein. The professor would periodically drop into the small auditorium for a few minutes. After such visits he would leave, unless his input was needed. I felt pretty intimidated there given that my understanding of the topics discussed was very poor. The subjects I learned at university were between fifty and two hundred years old, but the stuff we worked on in Krein's seminars was relatively modern—and I needed both time and a good mentor to catch up.

I told Vladimir Kostin about my participation in the seminar, and he was delighted. However, he said that he wasn't allowed to participate; the university Math Faculty didn't want any association with Professor Krein. When I asked why, Vladimir told me that, as he understood it, there were two main reasons: first, cooperation with Krein should lead to an invitation for him to work at the university (something that, on an ideological basis, the KGB wouldn't allow); and second, the dean of the Math Faculty wanted the department's research to align with Moscow State University's, not with Krein's. Vladimir and I thought these notions were strange: we believed that there are—or should be—no boundaries in math (for political—or any other—reasons). However, this was one of the oddities, or idiocies, of Soviet reality.

Ever since he'd introduced me to Krein's seminar, I'd been visiting Misha's home more frequently. One day, when I arrived, I found him sick in bed. He was typing something. When he showed me some pages, I realized that the font on his typewriter was very similar to the one used in the reference letter for emigration that Galina had typed for me. I produced my letter and asked Michael to key "to Israel" in the blank space. Initially, his answer was a resolute no. He explained that the KGB registered every typewriter in the Soviet Union and had a sample of the font used on each one. Therefore, the KGB could easily track him down if they suspected there was something fishy about my reference letter; it would endanger his job, career, and the well-being of his whole family. It was most certainly a terrible crime to use his typewriter for my fraudulent reference letter and I felt badly for asking. That said, these types of favors were not unusual in those days; still, looking back I appreciate the gravitas of the situation now so much more.

It took me a few weeks of begging and promising that I wouldn't compromise him for typing the two words into the letter. I believe that Misha spoke to his father-in-law, who assured him that I wasn't a KGB agent—after all, he had known my mother since they had sailed to and from Israel in 1967. Misha typed the words into the referral letter from the university, and my parents submitted our petition, along with all the other necessary papers. With trepidation, I awaited a call to the faculty office. They could expel me from the university, drag me through humiliating meetings, condemn me for treason, defiance of the Communist Party, and betrayal of the people of the Soviet Union. It could happen anytime. I was deathly afraid.

Meanwhile, almost all my marks in that year's summer exams were excellent (5). However, there were a few stressful moments in my exam on the final topics of the calculus course. The lecturer was Professor Eleonora Storojenko, a beautiful, intelligent, middle-aged woman with a reputation for being flirtatious. I answered all the theory questions, proved all the theorems, and solved all the problems. In the end, she announced my mark as 4 (80 percent). When I asked the reason for the grade, she said that I'd demonstrated knowledge of easy topics and solved easy problems; to get a higher score, I'd have to show more in-depth knowledge and ability.

After my experience with Professor Siniukov, I thought I was running into another antisemitic incident, but I decided to try anyway. I asked her for another round of questions and problems, more complex this time. I had no problem with the theory portion of the exam and solved one problem quickly. But the second problem was very difficult. I tried all the strategies I had learned from the Fikhtengol'ts books and other sources I'd slaved over during the previous two years; but it was a hard nut to crack. Then, when I realized that this problem might have no solution, and tried to prove it, I ran out of time. I presented the theory questions and the solved problem, and then I admitted that the last problem was very hard. I showed her my attempts and, telling her that I had a suspicion that the problem might have no solution, I demonstrated my work in that direction. Eleonora became very interested in how I proceeded, and in the end, she looked at me and said that she liked my perseverance and the set of tools I'd used for solving the last problem. She wrote "5" on my exam certificate—most certainly a hard-earned victory.

There were two kinds of yearly thesis projects: one for students who were starting to research the frontiers of math, the other for students who were streamed to the Computer Department or were on their way to become math teachers in junior high or high schools. My yearly thesis would lead to future research. I made my presentation to a committee of professors in an auditorium filled with a large group of students sitting behind the professors' desks. First, my mentor, Vladimir Kostin, gave an introduction, explaining to the committee how my thesis had been conceived and where it might lead in a few years. Then I presented what I was trying to achieve and the results that had come from my efforts. Professor Grabovskaya from our department then provided her opinion on the quality of my work. Finally, the committee awarded me a 5.

Galina's thesis was more straightforward. She had to review an article published in a math journal on an American mathematician's research. I had to work hard on this article to understand the background of the research, interpret the results, and provide my—Galina's—view on the value of the work. It wasn't easy, but at least it didn't require any creativity, just time. She got a 4 on "her" thesis and was pleased.

Fourth Year

In my fourth year, the men in our group continued to attend military training one day a week. In addition, we had to take a half-year "pedagogy of mathematics" course, since there was a deficit of math teachers in the Soviet Union. There was no final exam for this course; instead, we had to spend two months teaching math at a junior high or high school in the second part of the school year. The rest of the subjects were specific for each stream. My group—differential equations—studied theories of the mathematicians Aleksandr Liapunov and Henri Poincaré in depth, and participated in seminars given by our dean, Professor Gavrilov.

Much to my parents' chagrin, my middle brother Fima had run away from home to enroll in culinary school in Odesa. His dream was to travel the world as a chef on cruise liners. At the end of his studies, as a practice assignment, he worked in the cafeteria of a factory in Odesa. This was during the period when Sasha and I were spending every spare moment trying to bring our math knowledge up to the level we needed to pass. Every second day, Fima brought us a food package from the factory. It freed us from wasting time eating dinner at the student cafeteria and allowed us to spend more time studying. His help was vital and given from the bottom of his heart.

However, once he'd completed his studies, Fima found that he wasn't allowed to work as a chef on cruise liners—a predictable outcome, given his Jewish background. Instead, he was hired to work in the same factory cafeteria, serving breakfast and lunch to workers. His superior was Chef Aleksandr Ovsiannikov, a heavyset man of about fifty-five years old. He had to take insulin shots a few times a week and was missing three fingers on his right hand, which he had chopped off himself so that he wouldn't be drafted to the front lines during the Second World War. He and his wife lived in a one-bedroom apartment in the Moldovanka neighborhood of Odesa. Aleksandr, whom we called Uncle Sasha, liked working with Fima, who helped him from time to time and brought home some food from the cafeteria for him.

Fima told Uncle Sasha that I had served in the Red Army and was studying at university, and eventually introduced me to Uncle Sasha and his wife. They frequently invited me to their home for dinner. It was about fifteen minutes from my dormitory to their apartment in a small, typical Moldovanka backyard with many neighbors. Uncle Sasha would bring a piece of meat from the cafeteria and other items to cook for dinner. During dinner we would drink vodka or cognac and he would share his life story. He liked storytelling, and after a few drinks talked at length about his army life and how he'd guarded trains loaded with "enemies of the motherland" going to labor camps in Siberia. He also shared some of his adventures—such as "losing" his fingers to avoid serving in the front line or being the driver for his unit's commander while having a love affair with the man's wife.

Sometimes, after consuming a very large quantity of alcohol, he told stories about corruption in the food industry: supermarkets, restaurants, and cafeterias were all involved. For example, Uncle Sasha helped his bosses take food from the factory, and he had to compensate for meat, taken or stolen, with bread and pieces of fat. In return, his boss would close his eyes to Sasha's taking food home or exchanging it for needed supplies from the food store. It was a kind of barter market using stolen property. This system was practiced by most people in the Soviet Union, given their low wages. Uncle Sasha's stories brought to life—once again—the playful curse "May you live on your salary alone" and the common joke "The Communist Party and the government pretend that they pay people salaries; in return, people pretend that they work!"

Uncle Sasha drew back a curtain on what had previously been partially hidden to me: a glimpse into the widespread corruption in the whole Soviet economy. I had witnessed it to a degree in my day-to-day life, but this was a whole new level. His stories helped me understand that the whole country was in the hands of the communist mafia. The party created and sustained massive networks of economic corruption, along with a network of KGB agents everywhere who spied on everyone and controlled everything. It took a colossal military and police effort to protect the ruling regime and threaten the free world. The regime ideologically regulated the education system and all media channels. I had known this about life in the Soviet Union before, from my school years, but there were many unanswered questions in my mind in those days. Now, with Uncle Sasha, everything came together and left me with a coherent understanding.

One day I ran into Anatoly Glance, who had been in the army with me, in a candy store. He was there to buy a box of chocolates for his wife, and he invited me to come along with him to celebrate her birthday. After his discharge, Anatoly had found a job at the airport servicing jets; he had met his future wife at his workplace. He told me that the airport's runway was also used by the military and that unit was servicing and repairing military jets landing there.

His wife and her father also worked at the airport, and his wife's mother was a professor at Odesa's Academy of Agriculture. It was a friendly family; I visited them many times until Anatoly told me he was divorcing his wife. By that time, they had a little son, but something wasn't right between Anatoly and his wife. He also told me that his wife's family was quite antisemitic. Her parents had nudged her toward divorce by telling her that she'd made a mistake marrying a Jew. Indeed, Anatoly had often overheard her parents using antisemitic language. He went back to live with his mom in a building close to the House of Scientists on Gogol Street, not too far from the university. After that, I continued to meet with him from time to time.

I kept going to Professor Krein's seminars, but Misha Sonis came less regularly. After winter break, I had to spend about two months at a teaching practicum. Instead of being sent to teach in a village, I visited School Number 1 in Belgorod-Dnestrovsky, where I had studied before moving to the night school for working youth. I met with the school principal, Alexander Ogorodnikov, and the vice principal for the Math Department, and I received their okay to teach at the school for my practicum. I spent two months living at home with my parents and my siblings. My teaching at the school was difficult: I had a heavy load, checking students' homework, and leading some after-school activities. But being home with my family outweighed the hardships of that teaching venture.

Everything went smoothly except in one ninth-grade class, where a few students truly challenged me. The leader of the troublesome group was the son of another teacher in the school—my previous teacher, Joseph Greenspoon. The boy was very arrogant and would make nasty comments behind my back. I kicked him out of class once, hoping that he would come to his senses, but he continued his shtick during my lessons. One day he said something profane—which was too much for me to swallow. I left the classroom, returned with the vice principal, and asked the boy to repeat what he'd said. He put his head down and didn't say a word. Then I asked him to explain what I was doing to provoke his behavior. Again, he was silent. The vice principal took him out of class. A few days after this incident, he asked me to forgive him and let him sit in my math lessons. Although I felt that the boy wasn't sincere in his apology, my answer was that this would be fine—but only because of my deep respect for his father.

In the springtime my family received a negative answer to our petition to leave the Soviet Union and go to Israel. We filled out another application for emigration, then. My brother Fima returned home from Odesa and started working as a chef in a cafeteria in the city center, alongside our sister Emma. Izia continued his studies at the same high school I had attended and also at the city's music school. I was surprised that there was no action against me at university and that there had been no calls for meetings denouncing my desire to emigrate.

My Final Year

I returned to Odesa to attend university. Since Sasha had been accepted for computer studies, our schedules differed, and we didn't continue our work together. There were fewer subjects to study, and there was some obscure material that I didn't find appealing. However, I continued attending Professor Krein's seminars. I made a few friends among his doctoral students. I also noticed the absence of Misha Sonis. I assumed that he was sick, and I tried to visit him at home. Nobody answered the door, and the neighbors couldn't tell me where Misha and his family were. I approached the seminar leaders and asked them about him. They looked at me coldly and said that they didn't know. Misha and his family had disappeared, and nobody could tell me where they had gone. Initially, I thought that the KGB had arrested him for helping me with the reference letter for emigration, but this was unlikely because I hadn't been expelled from university (yet). Many, many years later we were reconnected and I learned that Misha had become a successful professor of mathematics in Israel and later in the USA. Thankfully, he was never punished for helping me - much to my enormous relief.

One evening, while I was reading a book in the dormitory, I heard yelling in the hallway. When I went out to check what was going on, a third-year student passed me with blood running from his nose. Farther down the hallway, there was a guy who, upon seeing me, shouted in my direction, "Hey, dirty Jew, get back to your room. You have no business being in this hallway!" I experienced a rush of unbridled energy in my legs; I simply couldn't handle hearing this guy hurl such insults at me. Without thinking, I ran at him and punched him hard in the face and chest.

His friends emerged and asked why I'd hit him. They told me that he'd had a few drinks, become very aggressive, and beaten up a student in their room. I informed them that if he, or anyone else, uttered the words "dirty Jew" when I was around, I would do the same thing to them. After I got back to my room, I met up with the fifth-year student who was also living there—Arkadi Weisman. He was a short, quiet guy who wore thick eyeglasses. He told me that I shouldn't have knocked the guy around in the hallway: he had been drunk and there might be repercussions. I had a difficult conversation with Arkadi: I told him that I had a low tolerance for antisemitic incidents like the one that had occurred that evening, that we should be proud to be Jews, and that we should not be afraid to defend ourselves. Arkadi tried to argue with me, but I was too upset with what had happened to listen to his weak arguments.

In June 1970, after I completed my fourth year, all of the men from my year were taken for summer military maneuvers near Chişinău, the capital city of Moldova. We were supposed to graduate after this as officers in the Red Army. For part of the summer, we were in barracks on the city's outskirts. After that, through the whole month of August, we were stationed in a forested area, providing communication lines to various army units participating in maneuvers. Most of the time, however, we weren't needed, so we were left to do whatever we wanted. I was a sergeant responsible for a platoon of mathematics and physics soldiers.

When we concluded our training at the end of August, each of us received an officer's certificate. We were ready to return to Odesa; but before we could begin our journey, we received news that the city had been shut down because of a cholera epidemic. Nobody was allowed to enter or leave Odesa. The earliest we could get back to university would be mid to late September. I was stuck in Chișinău. I spent a few days with my one-time neighbor, Stanislav (Stas) Manovski. His last name had been Kleiman when he lived in Belgorod-Dnestrovsky, he changed it to Manovski, his mom's maiden name, because it didn't sound Jewish. His mom was a Polish woman who'd married a Jewish man. Stas was teaching engineering at Chișinău's Construction College.

Stas's father was a senior engineer in a construction company in Belgorod-Dnestrovsky. They lived in the one-story building beside ours. Because of his position, Stas's father had a chauffeur who drove him in a black German limousine—a trophy brought in from Germany after World War II. As kids we'd loved to go around the block in this car. We also enjoyed Stas's birthdays because his mother and grandmother baked tasty cakes. He studied violin at the city's music school. They had much more money than we did; they were in our city's upper class. There was some animosity between Stas's mom and grandmother because his father was Jewish. However, they lived under the same roof, and we didn't hear many arguments between the women in the family.

Without warning, Stas's father was arrested and imprisoned for fifteen years. The construction company was missing lots of construction material; along with some other managers, he was accused of either stealing or negligence. Stas's grandmother died a few years after this happened. The city authorities split their apartment into two and gave half to another family. Stas's mother had never worked before her husband's arrest and imprisonment; now she had to work to support her family. During the years in which she worked in the city hospital's laundry department, my mom helped her as much as she could—sometimes with a bit of money, sometimes with some fish she brought from the fish factory. Stas was one year younger than me, but until he left Belgorod-Dnestrovsky to learn construction engineering, we were friends and just neighbors. When I wasn't able to return to Odesa after my summer military service in Chișinău, he accommodated me for a few days until I decided to travel to Moscow to see my old teacher from Belgorod-Dnestrovsky, Mark Geizer, I called my parents and told them that I was heading to Moscow until the cholera quarantine in Odesa was over.

When I arrived in Moscow, Mark told me that he'd changed his first name to Matvei, the Russian version of Matthew. I laughed and told Matvei that he couldn't hide his Jewishness. He explained that he needed a Russian name for his documents. He was planning to publish books and a Russian first name would help—a lot.

Mark had an apartment near the school where he worked as a math teacher. Every morning he would go to school and stay until about five o'clock. Afterwards, he had some homework to do that made him very tired by the evening. I found myself sitting in his apartment and cooking for him, and felt extremely bored. I often asked him to go downtown with me so that I could see the city, but he was exhausted. Two weeks after I'd arrived, the quarantine in Odesa was lifted, and I happily returned to university. Before I left Moscow, however, Matvei told me lots of his secrets. He confessed why he'd left Belgorod-Dnestrovsky, explained how he managed to stay in Moscow, and told me about his sexual escapades with his students' mothers in Belgorod-Dnestrovsky and women teachers in Moscow. He had something in him that attracted women, but he never committed himself to long relationships. Despite this, he told me that he planned to get married in the upcoming winter and asked if I would be his best man. I agreed.

I got back to Odesa at the end of September for the beginning of my last and final year. We still had some new subjects to learn, along with writing a master's thesis. I attended a few seminars with Mark Krein; the seminar would soon end. The manuscript he'd written was sent for publication; when it came out, I bought two copies—one for myself and one for Vladimir Kostin. Since I still hadn't seen Misha at the seminar, I asked another seminar leader, Dr. Daletsky, about my friend's whereabouts. He looked at me strangely, too, and told me that he honestly didn't know. Soon after that, I stopped going to the seminar.

After the winter exams, Matvei called to invite me to his wedding in Moscow. It was in the cold month of January 1971. Mary, Matvei's bride, was the daughter of a man who'd developed an underground facility to produce lipstick for women in Moscow. This man was arrested by the KGB and sentenced to death for economic crimes against the communist government. This was during Khrushchev's time, when the government was trying to suppress any private economic initiatives. Mary was a pretty and intelligent woman, slightly older than I was.

After their wedding, when I returned to Odesa, my parents had news for me. First, they had received another denial for emigration to Israel. Second, my sister Emma would be getting married in the early spring to a Jewish boy who was now at military school, preparing to become an officer in the Red Army. Third, my brother Fima had been drafted into the military for three years. My parents decided to apply again for emigration to Israel—despite the odds—and they asked me to help prepare for Emma's wedding. They also asked me if I could somehow buy some apparel in Odesa (long white gloves to match Emma's wedding dress, a tiara, and other items that were not available in Belgorod-Dnestrovsky).

These things were available in only one store in Odesa, and it was open only to foreigners and people working on Soviet cruise liners. No one could pay for the goods using regular Soviet money; it accepted only foreign currency or coupons given to workers on liners. But Yuri Matveev, in the Math Faculty, could help me: his father was a seaman in a fleet that hunted whales in Antarctica. Yuri sold me some coupons and took me to the store. The next time I visited my family, these special wedding goods for Emma made them very happy.

The wedding reception was in a restaurant on Belgorod-Dnestrovsky's main street. My parents had worked hard to pay for the party, and they were very proud of the event. There were lots of guests from the groom's side. They came from a small town called Artziz, about thirty-five miles from our town. The airbase with supersecret SU 9 jets was nearby; I felt a twinge of shame recalling that I'd wanted to do my two and a half years' service after basic training in Dniprodzerjinsk there, but had been denied security clearance because—no surprise—I was a Jew.

During the second part of my fifth year, I spent a significant amount of my time writing my master's thesis and reading and analyzing math publications for Galina's diploma.

Moving On

At the end of April, the fourth- and fifth-year students from the Math and Physics Departments who had studied French as their foreign language (I'd starting learning it at elementary school) were summoned to a meeting. We were informed that a French cruise ship was expected to arrive in Odesa, bringing a large group of tourists from France. These tourists obviously wouldn't speak Russian, and they needed interpreters. We were chosen to be tour guides and interpreters, and were given instructions and some training a few days before the ship arrived.

The evening before, one of my classmates, Oleg Brushchenko, knocked on the dormitory door. He called me into the hallway and told me that he was passing a message from the head of the university group assigned to help French tourists. My services wouldn't be needed, and I shouldn't come to the port the next morning. This was a big surprise to me, so I asked Oleg why. He couldn't look me in the eye and tried to avoid answering. However, after I pressed him, he asked me if my family had applied for emigration to Israel. I figured out two things: first, Oleg must have been cooperating with the KGB (or perhaps was actually a KGB agent) because he had access to this information; second, the officials at the university were clearly aware of my family's plan, but had (surprisingly) not punished me yet. I thanked Oleg for the message and wondered why the university bosses had decided not to expel me. All these years later, I still don't know.

A few weeks before I defended my master's thesis, during a visit to my parents, they asked me to help them with my brother Izia, then the only child still at home: I lived in Odesa; Hanna was completing her teaching work in a village; Fima was in military service somewhere in Kazakhstan; and Emma had followed her husband to his army base in the far east of the Soviet Union, near the border with China. Izia had just finished his violin studies at the city's music school—with good results—and he wanted to continue his musical education. Unfortunately, he was advised not to apply to Odesa's famous Stolyarsky music school because of its very low quota for Jews.

The only place he could be admitted was the music college in Severo-Donetsk—a coal mining city on Ukraine's northern border with Russia. Even there, admission required a sizable bribe. One of Izia's past teachers from the Belgorod-Dnestrovsky music school, Mark Levin, worked as a violin teacher at the Severo-Donetsk college. He advised my parents to send Izia with about six hundred rubles—approximately half a year's income for a worker. My mom had saved enough money; she asked me to take my brother there, pay the bribe, and ensure he was admitted. So Izia and I took a train to Severo-Donetsk, where we were met by Mark Levin. On the first day, Izia and I listened to the college students playing violin for their yearly exams. I gave an envelope with the money to Mark Levin, and the following day he told me that my brother would have to audition before a committee of teachers. After lunch, Izia played for the committee and got in. I settled him in the dormitory, left him some of my money, and took the train home. My parents were now in an empty nest, and, unbeknownst to him then, Izia was one milestone closer to his future at Buckingham Palace.

Izia and his wife Ani with Prince Charles (now King Charles III).

Soon after my trip to Severo-Donetsk, I defended my thesis before the university's math professors. It was easy and enjoyable; I felt lots of support from my mentor, Vladimir Kostin, and a few other professors who liked the results of my labors. I had a few more weeks before I was to receive my university diploma. Sadly, my friend Sergei, whose father was part of the communist group connected to the Math Faculty, told me that after graduation many students would be sent to remote villages to teach mathematics in elementary and high schools. I realized at that moment that I was likely to be selected for this "wonderful" opportunity.

Although I hoped that Vladimir Kostin would invite me to become a PhD candidate student under his supervision, which would save me from being sent away, I had serious doubts that it would happen. I became very anxious; I felt that it wasn't fair for me to sacrifice another three years of my life in some village. I badly wanted to get a PhD; it was a ticket to a better life and higher social status. I had to avoid teaching in a village. If I wasn't going to be a PhD student, the only other ways to stay in town were to be a computer science major, which I wasn't, or to get a freestanding master of mathematics diploma. I had to escape this predicament.

I came up with the idea of getting a medical certificate that would disqualify me from a teaching job. I had stuttered heavily in my childhood, and

I was sure that schools didn't want teachers with this deficiency. I made an appointment at the Odesa Psychiatric Clinic to be examined by the medical committee and had about six days to practice stuttering. I still had a very mild stutter, but this was insufficient. I stuttered in front of the mirror in the dormitory room for a week. I remembered which consonant sounds caused me the most problems, how to open my mouth, and how to move my head when stuttering. After a few days of practicing, I started stuttering as well as in my early days.

The psychiatric committee was composed of five medics. They asked me why I needed to see them. Demonstrating my heavy stutter, I told them honestly that the distribution of university completion diplomas was the following week. After that, we'd be sent to various schools to be teachers, and I was afraid that I wouldn't be able to do it because of my speech impediment. One committee member asked me why I was worried; the university officials would see and hear me stuttering and free me from any obligation to teach at school. I answered them that I wouldn't have asked for an appointment at the clinic if this were the case. There was strong demand for math teachers and the universities had to meet their quota. The members of the committee laughed at what I said; but after talking among themselves, they gave me a medical certificate for second-degree stuttering that included a strong recommendation that I shouldn't teach. I was overjoyed; I wouldn't have to leave Odesa.

A few days later, the university's academic committee had a special meeting to review referrals for all candidates for PhD programs. My friend Vova—who had finished his second year of doctoral studies in differential equations and worked as a TA—was on the committee. After the academic committee's meeting, he came to my dormitory and asked me to walk outside with him. He described what had happened during the meeting. Vladimir Kostin had presented my candidacy, explaining to the meeting participants that my master's thesis was already very close to becoming a PhD thesis and that I would only need to go through the formality of taking a few courses and running a few seminars for students. He gave me a glowing reference, but the attending representative of the KGB stopped him.

The KGB agent asked Vladimir why he was promoting future Zionist supporters, which would be tantamount to preparing math specialists for Israel. He challenged Vladimir's loyalty to the Communist Party and asked him if he fully appreciated the privilege of working at the University of Odesa. Vova told me that it was a pity to watch how Vladimir Kostin froze—mouth open, face pale, and unable to speak—after these remarks and barely veiled threats. The scene ended when Vladimir swiftly withdrew my candidacy. Vova was open with me: he said that there could be no future for me in this country and suggested that—if the opportunity was available—I should emigrate to Israel. He provided me with the moral support that only a best friend could. His words remain vivid in my mind; they will stay with me all my life.

A few days after I learned that I wouldn't be accepted into the PhD program, there was a final event at the faculty. All the students who had graduated from the math faculty in 1971 lined up to receive their certificates of completion or final diplomas, along with a document stating their place of work for the next three years. Each student's place in the line was based on their average mark on their exams; I stood in the first third. A committee of five or six university officials sat at a long, regal table from which, one by one, they would congratulate us on finishing university, shake our hands, and give our documents.

When I came up, after shaking hands, I stood in front of the official who handed me my papers and told me that I had been given the privilege of teaching math in a village quite far from Odesa. I thanked him, but I told him that I wouldn't be able to accept the position. He looked at me and asked what the problem was. I handed him the certificate I had obtained from the psychiatric committee. He looked at it, looked at me, and looked again at the certificate. Then he said, "Son of a bitch." He told me to come back in two weeks to get my university "free" diploma. A free diploma meant that I had to find a job by myself, that the university wouldn't send me anywhere.

I could only stay in the dormitory and in Odesa until mid-August. Of course, I hoped to find a suitable position with regular pay, which would allow me to stay and earn a living in Odesa while still having student status. The Soviet regime had turned every citizen into a serf: we were neither free to move from one location to another nor were we permitted to freely choose where to work. As I had learned before traveling to Moscow for my MGU interview, every Soviet citizen had to obtain an internal passport in which was a record of their places and dates of birth, their parents' names, nationalities (ethnicity), workplaces, and addresses. Each citizen had to be registered in the office of their communal block registry, which was supervised by the local police. In order to change addresses or move to another city, they needed a special permit from the registry. My permit to live in Odesa would expire at the end of August 1971 and I'd have to leave the city permanently. In order to stay in Odesa, I had to get a job and somewhere to live.

Toward the end of June, the dormitory emptied. Only one of my classmates, Vladimir (we called him Vovchik) Nikolaev, remained in my room. Vovchik received an assignment to work at the new computer center in a city close to his parents' home in the Crimea area. Over the previous two years, Sasha Svirski and I had taken care of Vovchik, mentoring him, providing him with food, and helping him with various other things. He had no family in Odesa and no other friends. He had been a classmate of Sasha's in the computer department.

On the last day of Vovchik's stay in Odesa, I asked him how he viewed me—both as a person and as someone with a Jewish background. I had sensed some undercurrents of negativity from him and could never quite pin it down; this conversation presented me with an opportunity to clear the air. I explained to him that I was Jewish and I had often been mistreated—by people and by organizations—because of my background. I was simply interested in why he had still interacted with me.

I was astonished to hear from him that he felt positively about me and that he appreciated all the help and attention he had received from me. However, he added that he would neither like to be friends with me nor to work with me. I asked him what I had done to encourage such sentiments in him. His answer was quite revealing. Vovchik told me that he was raised to suspect Jews of wrongdoing and believe that they should not be trusted. I asked him if he saw something in particular in me that confirmed that I was untrustworthy. What, I wondered, would prevent him from working with me? He answered that I was okay with him—no problem—but he wouldn't work with me because I was ambitious and pushy.

It certainly wasn't a happy conversation: this guy had lived in the same room with me for almost three years. It left me feeling incredibly sad and angry—yet another indication that Soviet life wasn't for me and that the friendships to which I had committed myself were tenuous. This encounter reinforced my burning desire to fight for a change in my life. The next day he left Odesa, and I never talked to him again. The last thing I learned about him was from Sasha Svirski: Vovchik married a year after leaving Odesa, had two children, and died in the nineties from pancreatic cancer.

I met with Anatoly Glance at the beginning of July and told him about my predicament. I had started looking for a position, but I also needed a stamp in my passport that certified that I legally resided in Odesa, at least for the time being. Anatoly told me that he might be able to help me, but asked me to be patient for a week.

Meanwhile, I started a job search. There were lots of factories and organizations in Odesa that needed mathematicians. Each time I would come to the human resources department and ask if they were looking for mathematicians with a university diploma, the first answer was yes. They would all give me an application form. Each form had a line asking my nationality/ethnicity, where I had to write that I was Jewish. After reviewing my application, the HR clerk would usually ask me to come the next day for the answer. I always had a negative response the next day: I was told that the position had been eliminated, had already been filled, or that the posting was a mistake (the company actually didn't need new mathematicians).

It was a very frustrating first week: I still hoped to find a job, but I recognized a pattern. There was a strong demand for mathematicians (it was prime time for the computerization of industries) and there weren't enough qualified people. Despite this reality, no company would hire a Jew. Or had I been blacklisted by the Odesa KGB?

My Fight for Freedom

I was beginning to lose hope when a woman who had graduated from the Math Department a year earlier knocked on my room, entered, and asked me if I had already found a job. After I said no, she told me that she was relieved because she had a message from her father, a professor in the Electrical Engineering Department at the Odesa Polytechnic Institute. He had two mathematicians working for him on research projects and as math tutors. They had completed their PhD studies, defended their doctoral theses, and gone to research labs in other cities. Her father had met with my mentor, Vladimir Kostin, who'd given me a glowing reference. The professor sent his daughter to offer me a role in his department. I passed my papers to the professor with some hope and waited for a meeting with him or a formal job letter.

The following week I kept searching for work, all the time expecting to hear from the Polytechnic. Nothing happened—until, that is, the professor's daughter came to talk to me in the middle of the second week. She looked scared; her gaze flitted around the room. She told me that I had put her father in a very awkward situation: he had submitted my papers to HR, but after a few days of waiting, he was called to HR, where he was met by a few KGB officers who had a lengthy conversation with him about hiring Jews and, in particular, me. The officers had scared her father by hinting that his job would be in danger if he tried to disobey their instructions. As had happened to my mentor Vladimir Kostin, they warned him not to prepare math specialists for Israel and, instead, to focus more on Ukrainians or Russians. Her father returned my papers and sent his profound apologies for the incident. He begged me to understand that he had no choice about who he could hire.

At that point I finally understood that there were absolutely no possibilities for me in Odesa. I continued going from place to place, but it only confirmed what I already knew. Meanwhile, Anatoly Glance managed to find a place where I could be registered as an Odesa resident. His grandparents lived in a three-room apartment in Moldovanka that was luxurious by Soviet standards. The authorities gave his grandparents the apartment because of their Bolshevik past. They had taken part in the revolution, were dedicated members of the Communist Party, and had held positions of authority for many years. Now they were old and frail, but they still believed in the ideals of communism and the leadership of the party. Anatoly loved them—despite their ideological differences—and they loved their only grandson.

The old pair agreed to sign me on as a resident and arrange for the registrar to put a stamp in my passport certifying that I lived legally in their apartment (it cost me ten rubles to bribe the registrar). However, the old folks didn't really want me to live with them in their apartment. I quickly found a room for rent just a block away from them on Hvorostina Street, not far from Evreiskii (Jewish) Hospital, an institution in Moldovanka. My room was in an apartment owned by a woman who rented out two rooms. Three working-class guys lived in the second room. They walked through my room to get to their place, so I didn't have much privacy. I made a curtain around my bed and organized my stuff there. Some days I still slept in the dormitory and other days in my new "apartment."

One evening I was called to the telephone in the dormitory, which was on the guard's desk. The call was from one of my university classmates. She asked me if I had landed a job yet. She told me that a new organization was working on automating information processes in several heavy industry factories in Odesa. They were desperate to find useful people. The next day I took a streetcar there. It was located in a large factory, about twenty minutes away. When I arrived at the offices, I had to go through the normal process, telling the HR person about myself and filling out the application form. I was asked to come back in two days.

When I returned, I was met by a guy who presented himself as Tovarishch [comrade] Ivanov, head of the Communist Party for the organization. He took me to a meeting room and called in the boss, Viktor Klimov. I sat across the table from them—ready to hear the reasons for rejecting me. Instead, Ivanov started to explain the purpose of the work and Odesa's branch of Kharkiv's Institute for the Automation of Heavy Industry Factories. Their tasks included implementing computers for management processes and supporting other control technologies for managing physical processes in factories. He cited a few successes of the mother organization in Kharkiv and talked about a bright future ahead for the Odesa branch. He also presented Viktor Klimov to me; he'd earned his engineering degree from the Institute of Communications in Odesa. Ivanov told me that Viktor would be a great boss, but that his directorship position was contingent on him finishing his PhD on the automation of management systems.

Viktor was writing his thesis; however, he had been struggling with math. The conversation then turned to my potential employment. Viktor and Ivanov told me that they'd spent two days reviewing my résumé and talking to people at my university to obtain references. They told me that they were aware of my difficulties getting a job and that they were willing to risk taking me on, if, that is, I agreed to their terms. This was encouraging. Ivanov and Viktor asked me to keep the terms secret.

They told me that Vladimir Kostin assured them that I could tackle the math section of Viktor's thesis. They would offer me a job in the company if I agreed to help Viktor out while doing my regular job duties. It was a terrible moment for me, but I had no choice, so I agreed. The conditions of my employment made it perfectly clear that I would never be able to do a PhD in the Soviet Union and wouldn't be able to build a career there. Instead, in exchange for a low-paying job, I would be used by people in power to provide them with my skills to improve their lives and careers. Such was the price for being a Jew in the Soviet Union.

My role was to supervise a small group of young specialists who had finished studying in various higher education institutions in Odesa. Since none of them had served in the army, they all were younger than me. And they had no experience working with computers, which was quite common in 1971. We sat in the main office (located at the factory) for a few weeks, where we were given all kinds of assignments unrelated to the project we were to launch in September. Meanwhile, new employees were still being hired for the team.

Our head, a scientific leader, was a woman who had finished her education at the Polytechnic Institute's Management Faculty. She was part of the decision-making team in the organization—Ivanov, Viktor, and herself. At first, I thought that the initial assignment was serious and important. I don't remember the nature of my first small project, but I finished it in two days, producing a set of diagrams and explanations. When I showed her, she looked at the material and said, "Roman, you don't understand. I gave you this assignment to work on for a week. You're rushing. Come back to me at the end of this week." After speaking with a few guys on my team, I realized that management wanted us to pretend to be busy until they formulated our big project and got approval from the head office in Kharkiv. So we spent our time playing cards when there were no supervisors around and pretending we were working hard when they were present. This continued until mid-September.

Our project was formalized and approved in September. My team was sent to a small factory that produced spare parts for other factories. Our task was to study every department's information flow: reports, invoices, financial controls and reporting, HR, and so on. Every morning, I would send my people to various departments, telling them to collect all the paperwork, count the number of words and the numerical calculations, and explain the formulas for calculations and the processes' logic. My group's results had to be tabulated and recorded in a long and tedious report. With this information, we could discern the order of magnitude of information flow in the factory and estimate the computing power needed to automate it. After giving my team their tasks, I would go to the city library to work on Viktor's doctoral thesis.

One day Viktor invited me to his place for dinner. He, his wife, and his mother lived in an apartment on Peter the Great Street, a street which I had walked along for a few years, from the dormitory to the university and back. Their building was close to the Odesa Central Post. Viktor's mother was a nice Jewish woman; in fact, I felt that she embodied the quintessential Jewish mother in the Soviet Union: she was very warm and welcoming, she hovered over her child and his friends, and she was always in the kitchen making food. Viktor's father wasn't Jewish; he had left his family a long time ago. We had a nice dinner, and we talked about the schedule for Viktor's doctoral thesis. I promised him it was reasonable and that I'd found lots of material on his subject in the library.

There, I had read interesting work in math done in the United States in the 1930s. The Americans had designed optimal management processes, technology to support these processes, and had developed some mathematical underpinnings for them. This was everything Viktor needed for his dissertation—except some modern mathematical models and computer technology. I saw how I could borrow from these early works and combine the pieces with mathematical theory, including probability, linear algebra, calculus, and differential equations. (In the meantime, in September, my family was again denied emigration to Israel. My parents applied again.)

One evening after work, Galina Kirova came to visit me in my apartment. It was a friendly meeting, but she begged me to help her with her work assignment. Somehow, she also had received a free diploma from university and avoided being sent to a village to teach math. Instead, she'd been hired by a secret "closed" office working on military projects; we called such organizations "postal boxes." Because of my Jewishness, I was excluded from these well-paying organizations. But people there were quite restricted; they were watched carefully by the KGB.

Galina worked on a project related to satellites and communications from space to Earth. Her latest assignment required solving a problem demanding good knowledge of differential equations and theories of stability. Since she couldn't leave me her work papers, I sketched out a strategy for solving her problem, estimated the time needed for more research, and promised to have some answers for her in a week.

Here I was, doing math work for two projects—Viktor's and Galina's—that were not my own, while I desperately wanted to be working on my own PhD. I became so angry and upset that I decided to join a Jewish dissident movement in Odesa to fight for the right to emigrate to Israel. It was dangerous, perhaps even reckless, but I was at my wit's end. On Friday evenings and Saturdays, I started going to the only operating synagogue in Odesa (the Soviet government had turned all the others into gyms or libraries). It was so new to me, and as much a moment of rebellion as capitulation—or maybe the beginning of a newfound energy to fight for justice in my own life. I had no way of knowing then that, a few months later, I would be on a train heading out of the Soviet Union. Getting there would require a good deal of determination, the help of friends, and a fortunate confluence of events.

CHAPTER 5

Hunger for Freedom

The functioning synagogue was in Peresip, a section of the city that was far from the center and, like Moldovanka—described so vividly in Isaak Babel's *Odessa Stories*—had been ruled by bandits and thieves before and during the Bolshevik Revolution. In the 1970s, the area was working class and still dangerous after dark. The synagogue was near the railroad that bordered Peresip, in an area that was considered a little better. I heard that a group of Jewish youth were congregating there to socialize, share information about Israel, and discuss strategies for leaving the USSR. It was precisely what I wanted!

At first, I wasn't accepted there by the regulars, who suspected me of being either a KGB agent or a collaborator. KGB men were regularly stationed around the synagogue area; they probably took pictures of everyone going in and coming out. I tried to talk to a few people, but they didn't display any desire to forge a friendship. On Saturday mornings, I would go up to the synagogue's second-floor balcony to see how a group of old Jews, about fifteen men in tallits (prayer shawls), were praying, removing a Torah scroll from a cabinet, and reading it aloud. I didn't understand anything they were saying, reading, or singing. It was all new to me. How strange to be a Jew and know so little about one's own traditions and roots. There were prayer books in Hebrew. It was all so foreign to me because I had been isolated from the Jewish religion all my life and, like most Jews of my generation, had almost no knowledge of the language, religion, customs, or culture. All these new discoveries were dangerous and no doubt placed me in harm's way with the KGB.

I was surprised to see a Ukrainian man sitting on the balcony praying in Hebrew from a prayer book handwritten in Ukrainian using the Russian alphabet. He told me that he was a member of a Christian sect that believed in the Old Testament and observed most of the rules of the Jewish religion.

Members of his sect would come to synagogue and pray in Hebrew to the same God as Jews. They were not allowed to practice on the main floor, so they sat in the women's section. He was way ahead of me in his belief in the God of Torah and observance of the commandments. I was shocked that there were groups who were not Jews who chose to associate with Jews. It was such a risk!

One day I approached a small group of Jewish guys in the synagogue's backyard and presented myself. After hearing my last name, one of them showed some interest in me. He said that his last name was also Rashkovsky and that his name was Izia. I told him about my younger brother Izia and my other siblings Hanna, Fima, and Emma. He warmed to me and said that he had a sister named Hanna as well. It was a surprising coincidence. From that day on, he was my guide to the synagogue.

He promised to introduce me to some important players in their group. Eventually, I got to know Katya Palatnik, whose famous sister Raiza was imprisoned for her desire to emigrate to Israel and for distributing religious literature and samizdat. I also got to know the two brothers Averboukh (Isai and Alex), the brothers Khazin (Mark and Igor), and others whose names I don't remember now. Gradually, they accepted me, and from mid-October I volunteered to sign their petitions to the government, demanding the right to emigrate: "Let My People Go." They had contacts with Western journalists in Moscow, and they passed on information about the KGB's and police's opposition to us. I was thrilled! I signed everything to get my name known in the West. Many articles have been written about the Palatnik sisters.[1]

One Friday evening, after prayers, as I started going home along a dark street, I noticed that two men wearing fur hats were following me. I turned into a narrow passage and started running. They gave chase and, as they closed on me, I realized that they were either KGB or bandits. I knew this could only end badly. When I'd nearly reached a decent area, I turned into

---

1   See, for example, Jane P. Shapiro, "The Politicization of Soviet Women: From Passivity to Protest," *Canadian Slavonic Papers* 17, no. 4 (1975): 596–616, https://www.jstor.org/stable/40866958; "The Stories They Tell: Raiza Palatnik," University of Southampton Special Collections, August 28, 2020, https://specialcollectionsuniversityofsouthampton.wordpress.com/2020/08/28/the-stories-they-tell-raiza-palatnik/; and "The Secrets of Israel," Let Our People Go, accessed November 26, 2023, https://m.facebook.com/sovietjewry/photos/raize-palatnik-prisoner-of-zion-1970-1972on-december-1-1970-palatnik-was-arreste/828777907519990/?locale=zh_CN.

a backyard that had two rear exits. I picked one and found myself in a dark and narrow passage. I was suddenly at the intersection of Deribasovskaya and Red Army, where I jumped on the first streetcar I saw, and in thirty minutes I was back in my room on Hvorostina Street. Never again did I stay late at the synagogue!

Many Jewish youths gathered at the synagogue on the Jewish holidays that fall: Rosh HaShana, Yom Kippur, and Sukkot. They were nicely dressed as they danced and sang songs in Yiddish and Hebrew. It was here that I first heard the lovely melody of "Yerushalayim Shel Zahav" (Jerusalem of Gold), written at the time of the Six Day War by the Israeli composer Naomi Shemer.

By now I was entirely accepted into the Jewish dissident movement. Some of the core members were young; one girl was in tenth grade in high school. She asked me to help her with math, so I did some tutoring without taking money for my time and effort. I also got closer to the Averboukh brothers and Katya Palatnik. Katya's focus was to help her sister Raiza get out of prison. She wrote frequent petitions to the KGB and sent copies to a few foreign journalists accredited in Moscow. They then sent these petitions to the Voice of America and Radio Free Europe. Whenever it was possible to listen to these stations (the Soviet Union tried to distort radio signals from the West), we heard Katya and her stories about her sister. I was so impressed by her commitment to freedom and justice. At the time I had little knowledge of the pressure groups (ex. "The 35s") that were being established as far away as London and New York City to lobby Western governments to help Raiza and other refuseniks - likely thanks in large part to Katya's efforts.

Later in life I learned that there was a group of young Canadians who were supporting the effort to free us and were involved in these radio broadcasts and protests in North America. Strangely enough, one such young man, David Sadowski (involved in the North American "Freedom Caravan for Soviet Jews" in 1971), would eventually become a senior executive at Toronto's United Jewish Appeal and, in that capacity, rent space to my daughter in connection with a dream I didn't realize I had quite yet. My improbable life, being improbable, contained many of these incomprehensible connections, twists, and miracles.

At the beginning of November, we started sending our group petitions, signed by our core participants, to the KGB and OVIR, an office for issuing exit visas. We sent copies to Moscow, Voice of America, and Radio Free Europe. We heard our names on the airwaves. It was incredibly risky— imprisonment, public ridicule, the Gulag, even death could follow. Still, as nobody at my workplace knew about my activities, I could continue as a group leader and PhD researcher for Viktor Klimov.

Hunger Strike

In mid-November, we started planning a demonstration and hunger strike in front of Odesa City Hall on Primorski Boulevard. We were going to stop eating for as long as it took, even if it killed us. And it was politically dangerous. However, we were informed by Western journalists stationed in Moscow that the Soviet Union was negotiating a deal with the United States for purchasing a large quantity of American wheat. President Richard Nixon had placed a condition on the deal—the Soviet Union had to ease restrictions on Jewish emigration. This made us believe that we had a real chance to get our exit visas! With the hunger strike coming up, I think I ate, drank, and dreamed of freedom each and every day, and had adrenaline for dessert.

We chose December 5—Soviet Constitution Day. People were allowed to submit petitions to the Soviet Supreme Court on the fifth, petitions that ranged from complaints about housing to reports of wrongdoing by officials. Unfortunately, the day happened to fall on a Sunday, so we postponed until December 6, which would be a proper working day. We planned to go to Odesa City Hall on Monday morning, deliver the petition, start the hunger strike, and erect signs that read "Let My People Go." The international Jewish movement in the West used the same slogan to help Soviet Jews emigrate to Israel. That said, for context, prior to Nixon's policy of détente during the Cold War, the annual number of Soviet Jews "permitted to leave" (i.e. exiled as traitors) for Israel was counted in (paltry) hundreds. There were several million Jews in the USSR at that time. The numbers were not in our favor.

To protect ourselves against possible arrest and imprisonment, we decided to contact the Western journalists we knew in Moscow; we passed along the names of everyone involved in the demonstration. We knew that having our names broadcast on radio stations in Europe and published in American and European newspapers could cause problems for the Soviets in their negotiation to buy wheat from the United States. Harvests on Soviet collective farms were terrible in 1971. There was a severe need for bread and other food items. So, while we were taking a real risk, there was also the possibility that we would succeed. We also heard from the journalists that some Jews from Georgia and western Ukraine were receiving exit visas. Perhaps it was because they lived on the periphery and hence wouldn't stir things up in large city centers; perhaps because they were stereotyped as hot-tempered and less educated, the government felt less inclined to keep them in the country. There was a solid Jewish dissident movement in Moscow and Leningrad, too. This news inspired us.

On Sunday, December 5, twenty-five of us met at the synagogue. We signed the petition and agreed to meet at 10:00 a.m. the next day at the entrance to City Hall. On Monday morning, I gave out the assignments for the day to my team members. Instead of going to the library to work on Viktor's PhD, I met our assembled group; we entered the building and stood in the entrance hall. There was an information and registration desk behind a glass wall. A middle-aged woman sat there and asked what we wanted. I was standing beside Katya Palatnik as she handed our petition to the woman. The woman read the petition, looked at us, and then read the paper again. She asked us to wait while she took our petition to the authorities. A minute later, a few policemen arrived and blocked the exit door. We were trapped.

Ten minutes later, a City Hall official appeared and invited all of us, twenty-five youths, to a large meeting room on the ground floor. We took seats around a long oval meeting table and were told to wait for the relevant city authorities. About half an hour later, two colonels in uniform entered the room. One was from the police—he was the head of the OVIR—and the other was from the KGB. The KGB officer started speaking first; he read our names from the petition we'd handed in earlier and demanded that we abandon our planned hunger strike. He promised that there would be no punishment and we would be free to go home. He also promised terrible repercussions if we didn't comply.

After we refused, the OVIR colonel gave us a long lecture on how inappropriate it was to think about leaving our Soviet paradise for Israel, that aggressor capitalist country, a puppet of America. He reminded us that the motherland had invested a fortune into our education and upbringing, how much better life in the Soviet Union was than in the rotten West, and how our departure would negatively impact our friends and families left behind. After a few hours of futile attempts to change our minds, the two colonels became quite agitated. They swore at us and threw insults. When they realized that they were not gaining ground, they changed their tune and threatened us with lifelong imprisonment and Siberia. We knew they were serious.

We sat for many hours at the table listening to these tirades. Police guarded us when we went to the washroom. The colonels tried to talk to each of us individually, with no result. When the sky became dark in the early evening, as usual in early December, the KGB colonel informed us that he would order a bus to take us to the Odesa prison.

At that point, Katya said that this outcome would be very damaging for the Odesa KGB and the Soviet government. The colonel was speechless for a few minutes, but then he started yelling and swearing at her, and demanded an explanation. She calmly explained to him that we'd communicated with Western journalists and passed them our names and plans for the hunger strike. We'd also alerted these journalists to expect a phone call before midnight to tell them what had happened today. If we didn't call them, they would tell the Western media about us. Katya went on to tell the colonels what would happen if we were arrested: America wouldn't sign the contract for selling wheat to the Soviet Union, which would harm the whole country. And Moscow would come down hard on Odesa's KGB for causing such a disaster.

Katya's explanation cooled the KGB agent's anger, and both colonels left the room. Only a few policemen remained. Close to 11:30 at night, the colonels returned. The KGB agent was furious and just swore a bit. But the OVIR colonel was more relaxed and told us that our wishes to go to Israel had been granted; we could come to his office the next day to start the paperwork. The KGB colonel yelled that we had ten days to leave the country, throwing in a few threats. It was awful and wonderful all at the same time.

We had won and they had lost! Our group agreed to leave City Hall together to avoid any provocation from the police or KGB. We suspected there would be violence against us. I asked my friends to wait for me, as I needed some clarifications from OVIR. I approached the colonel and asked him if he was personally familiar with my family's emigration applications. He answered affirmatively after learning my last name. My question was whether an exit visa would be granted to me only or to my parents and siblings as well. The colonel said that the whole family could leave the country. I asked him about my brother Fima who was serving in the army in Kazakhstan. Will he be released from his service to emigrate with our family? The answer was positive. I felt like a heavy weight was lifted from my shoulders. We left the building close to midnight. Katya rushed to call the journalists in Moscow to inform them of our victory.

The next day, I took a day off and took a train to Belgorod-Dnestrovsky to see my parents. They were surprised to see me, but when I told them that we were all free to go to Israel, they were overjoyed. My mom cried, my father pulled out the vodka, and we drank "L'Chaim."

Early the next morning, my father and I went to Odesa. We arrived at the OVIR offices at around ten in the morning. There, we had to wait for about half an hour to be received by the clerk. After we presented ourselves, she took us to the colonel's office. He was somber, but he greeted us politely. He gave us forms for emigration, and I asked him again if we should include all our family members in the application form. The colonel asked us to wait for a few minutes and left his office. When he returned, he apologized and said that our entire family was entitled to emigrate except my brother Fima because he was serving in the army. I was surprised and reminded him about his promise a day ago when he said that Fima can also leave with the family. The colonel apologized again and said that he made a mistake after a long and challenging day dealing with our group. Fima couldn't go. Then my father said that he needed to talk to my mom before filling the form as he foresaw some serious problems with leaving the country without his son.

I asked the colonel if it would be possible that only part of the family would leave the country because of Fima, and the rest would emigrate after Fima completed his service. The answer was positive. The other question I asked was about how much time we were given to leave the country. A day ago, the KGB colonel said that we had only ten days, but I would need a few more because of all the chores I had to do regarding personal documents, payments to the government, and resigning from work. Again, the OVIR colonel said that I could take as many days as needed, but not too long. He added that I must be out of the country by the first week of January, 1972.

My father left Odesa for Belgorod-Dnestrovsky, but I stayed in Odesa as I needed to resign from my job, and I wanted to meet a few of my close friends. I picked up the papers I wrote for Viktor Klimov and went to the office.

Viktor was sitting in his office alone when I walked in. I closed the door and told him that I was resigning because I was emigrating to Israel. He sat quietly and looked at me. I gave him a stack of papers I wrote for his dissertation and asked if I could walk him through my work. He nodded, and we spent about an hour together. After that, he gave me the required paper to prove to OVIR that I had properly resigned from my job. Then I left without shaking his hand. I knew that he didn't want to shake my hand, and he wanted me to leave the premises as quickly as possible. It was an uncomfortable meeting. The whole situation was sad and sour.

The same day, I met with Anatoly Glance. He told me that he envied me for leaving the country, but he was staying behind. He couldn't even think about leaving because he had divorced his wife and his baby son was in her custody. He had won the right to visit his son periodically and couldn't leave him fatherless. Anatoly asked me not to communicate with him from abroad—that would make his life inconvenient because the KGB screened all letters coming into the country and listened to all telephone conversations. I promised not to cause him problems when I was in Israel.

Next, I met with Vova Pavliuk and Boris Repinski. We sat in a small cafeteria where we could drink wine. As we were sitting and drinking, I informed my friends that I was in the process of leaving for Israel. Vova was very happy for me but asked me not to communicate with him from Israel because of his PhD studies and his work at the university as a TA. Boris became very angry and agitated. Later that evening, Vova explained that Boris had joined the Communist Party and become very loyal to the Party. Boris called me a traitor and hurled some swear words at me. I was very disappointed with him when we parted. After that, Vova walked with me to the bus station. I took the last bus to Belgorod-Dnestrovsky that evening.

I came home at night when everyone was already asleep. The following day, we had a long discussion about what we had to do, given the circumstances. First, my parents told me that they couldn't leave Fima behind. If they emigrated now, they would have to surrender our apartment to the government, then Fima wouldn't have a place to return to after his army service. The government could send him to a remote place after his army service so that it would be impossible to communicate with him. He would be stuck there for a long time, maybe for life. In addition, Izia just started violin studies in Severo-Donetsk, and my father wanted him to continue his studies. So, my parents said that I had to go to Israel with my sister Hanna. They would stay put until Fima completed his military services. Hanna agreed to this scenario.

Now we had to find a solution to another problem. Hanna and I had to pay approximately 1,100 rubles each to secure our exit visa: 500 to reimburse the Soviet Union for our education, and 600 for renouncing our citizenship. On top of this amount, there were other expenses for document translation, notarial services, currency exchange at the Moscow Bank (100 US dollars each), transportation out of the USSR (Odesa–Moscow–Vienna), and more. The two of us needed about 2,500 rubles in total, an astronomical amount of money we didn't have. At the time, this figure represented more than two years' salary of an engineer with a high level of education.

The whole concept of paying for renouncing our citizenship was absurd—but of course, not in the Soviet Union. Repayment for our education was also grotesque. My parents worked hard all their lives and received miserable pay for their work; the difference between what they were paid and what they should have received was the amount the Soviet government appropriated (stole) from them. Our family lived in poverty, lacking food, clothes, and other essential items, because the government cheated my parents out of an amount of money an order of magnitude greater than the cost of our education.

However, to leave the country, we had to find money to pay for our freedom. I contacted a few of my friends in Odesa who had also received the go-ahead to leave the country. They suggested that I travel to Moscow and go to the Dutch embassy, which had been representing Israeli interests since the Soviet Union broke diplomatic relations with Israel after the Six Day War. My friends told me that the Dutch embassy was lending money to Jews who had received permission to leave the country but didn't have money to repay their education and renounce citizenship. And so, I had to go to Moscow.

Fleeing Communism

I returned to Odesa to prepare our documents. It took me a day to find a translator for our papers, but I learned that notarial services for people leaving the country could be performed only in Kyiv, the capital city of Ukraine. While dealing with the translator for the next few days, I also started thinking about what I would need to do in Moscow to get the money required to pay the KGB, OVIR, and other authorities. My first thought was to call Mark Geizer on the phone from Odesa Central Post. Mark told me that he couldn't accommodate me at his place for a few days because of some family issues. Then, I tried my second option: I called Jacob's parents. I didn't tell them why I was going to Moscow; I only asked them if I could sleep at their place for a few nights. They were happy to help me with that. Two days later, when all our papers were translated into English, I bought a ticket to travel to Moscow by train. Before going to the train station, I stopped at the Odesa Post building and sent a telegram to Jacob: "To Agent #1: Agent #2 is arriving tomorrow at 7 pm. Please meet him."

Jacob's parents met me at the train station in Moscow and brought me to their apartment. We couldn't talk much in the taxi, but they scolded me for sending a strange telegram to Jacob. They told me they received a phone call from the police asking them who Agents #1 and #2 are. After learning that it was a game their son was involved in, nothing serious, the police stopped their phone conversation. I profusely apologized for the stupid telegram, and the conversation moved to other topics. After eating supper, I told them what brought me to Moscow. This frightened them even more, as they realized that I might be watched or even followed by the KGB and they might be blacklisted for helping a Zionist. But then they calmed down and whispered their confession: in fact, they envied me for my exit to Israel. They begged me not to cause any problems in Moscow as it would harm them by association. I promised I would behave.

The next morning, I called Mark Geizer, and he asked me to meet him before going to the Dutch embassy. We met in the city center, and he asked me to meet a friend of his who needed my help. Mark took me to the apartment of Leonid Frank and his mother Tzilia Moiseevna. Leonid studied math at Moscow University, completed his master's degree, and a few years later completed his PhD studies. He worked as a mathematician in the Moscow Institute of Aviation and Space. We had a cup of tea together while Leonid explained that he had applied for an exit visa to Israel, and there was a good chance that he would be able to leave the country.

Knowing that I was about to go to the Dutch embassy, Leonid asked if I could take some of his math research papers with me and request that the embassy officer send these papers to Israel. Leonid was sure that the KGB wouldn't let him take his research work with him out of the USSR. He would retrieve the papers when he arrived in Israel. Since he was introduced to me by my friend Mark Geizer, he trusted me. I agreed. Then both Mark and Leonid walked with me to the block where the Dutch embassy was located. For the last 200 meters I walked alone to the gates of the embassy. The guard at the gate asked me what I was doing there, and I showed him the document from Odesa OVIR confirming that I had permission to emigrate to Israel. I told the guard that I had personal issues to discuss with the embassy officers. The guard called somebody on the phone, and after a few minutes he let me in.

Somebody from the embassy met me at the door. As we entered, I presented my papers to the embassy representative and explained my financial problems. After waiting some twenty minutes, I was given the money needed, and I was asked if I needed more help. I said yes, but they started whispering to me to be quiet and took me to a small meeting room where we could speak freely. I told them about Leonid's request and gave them his research papers.

They checked every page, and then I gave them Leonid's name and some other information they asked me. The representative put Leonid's papers into a plastic pouch and attached a form with Leonid's name and other necessary information. We shook hands, and I walked out with the substantial amount of money required to get out of the USSR.

Mark and Leonid were waiting for me a few blocks from the embassy. After I met with them and Leonid thanked me for the help, he left us. I walked with Mark to have lunch in the cafeteria. I asked Mark if he could let me and my sister Hanna stay at his place on my last day in the Soviet Union before taking a train to Vienna. Mark said that this wouldn't be possible as his apartment was a one-bedroom place, but he promised to talk to his mother-in-law who might be able to accommodate us for one night. We agreed that I should call him on the phone from Odesa a week from then.

In the evening, I returned to Jacob's parents' apartment. I informed them that my visit's mission was accomplished and I would go home tomorrow. We had a pleasant, quiet conversation about Jewish life in the Soviet Union and about Israel, and they wished me a good life there.

They were not yet ready to take the risk of applying for permission to leave the USSR. The main reason was that their brilliant and talented young son was doing very well in school. They weren't sure that they could get an exit visa quickly, and they could lose their jobs and be kicked out of their apartment. Further, at their age, they imagined it would be hard to learn a new language and integrate into Israeli society. In short, they were afraid, and I understood their reasoning well.

We said goodbye to each other in the morning; there were hugs and best wishes for my new life in the Holy Land. I had a few more chores in Moscow before taking an afternoon train to Kyiv. Every Jew leaving the Soviet Union had the right to exchange 100 rubles for 95 dollars, so for myself and Hanna, I needed to exchange 200 rubles. The only place where it was possible to do this legally was the Moscow International Bank. In those years, banks were under complete governmental control and did not serve regular citizens; companies paid worker salaries in cash. Only a few large cities had government banks to deal with the needs of foreigners like journalists, tourists, and people traveling abroad on government permits.

It was about lunchtime when I arrived at the bank. I registered at the entrance and told the clerk of my needs. The clerk told me to take a seat in the waiting area and that I would be called soon. In about half an hour, I heard my name announced from a loudspeaker. I approached the teller's window and presented my emigration documents, and then the teller exchanged my rubles for dollars with surprising speed and efficiency.

I put the dollars into my bag and went to the exit. A young guy who looked like a Jew approached me and asked if I was Roman Rashkovsky. I confirmed that I was and asked him how he knew my name. He said that he was sitting in the waiting area and heard my name on the loudspeaker. He saw me going to the teller's window and was waiting for me. He presented himself as Vladimir M., a name quite familiar to me. I asked him if his name was broadcast a few times on Radio Free Europe as a member of a Moscow Jewish dissident movement. He confirmed this, and in turn asked me if I was from Odesa. I confirmed that too. We sat down in the corner of the waiting area to have a private conversation.

Vladimir told me that his mother was flying to Israel through Vienna in a few hours, and she needed some money. Vladimir asked me if I could lend him 100 rubles to buy US$95 for his mom. At first, I was taken aback, but Vladimir explained that they were driving to the airport and stopped at the bank to exchange money when Vladimir realized that he had left his cash at home. Now there wasn't enough time to go home and back to the bank as his mom would miss her flight. They desperately needed one hundred rubles.

Vladimir promised that he would give me my money back the next day. I explained to him that I would be in Kyiv the next day and then in Odesa to prepare for my own departure to Israel. I also told him that my sister and I needed money to buy tickets to travel by train from Odesa to Moscow, and after that from Moscow to Vienna. Vladimir became visibly desperate. Feeling his pain, I opened my bag and pulled out the 100 rubles for him. He hugged me and promised to send 100 rubles to my parents in a few days. I wrote my parents' address for him; he ran to exchange money for dollars.

This was an incredible risk. My freedom, my entire future, rested on the word of a stranger. I had no idea why I trusted him, but I did. He did indeed return the money to my parents. But what transpired between us surprisingly didn't end there. What unfolded with Vladimir—a chance meeting that turned into so much more in the years that followed—is beyond explicable. In the meantime, I took a taxi to the train station, where I bought a ticket for the evening train to Kyiv. After eating a sandwich at the station cafeteria, I called Mark Geizer to confirm that my sister and I would have a place to sleep on January 2, 1972. He confirmed that this would indeed be possible.

The overnight train to Kyiv was packed with all kinds of people. In my car, people were drinking vodka, playing cards, and talking the whole night—and doing so quite loudly. I had lots of money in my bag and was afraid of being robbed. I couldn't sleep and held my bag tightly to my chest, resting it on my knees. The train arrived in Kyiv in the morning; I didn't feel tired because of all the stress I had experienced in the last two days. I took a taxi to the Ukrainian Ministry of Justice and spent a few hours getting notarial approval on all the documents translated into English in Odesa. That was straightforward and, in the afternoon, I took a train to Odesa.

The train arrived in the morning. I came to the OVIR office to pay off our "debt" for education received in the Soviet Union and renounce citizenship for both Hanna and myself. I had with me two passport-sized photos for each of us as requested by OVIR. The OVIR colonel asked me about my parents and siblings and why they were not joining us. I told him that they didn't have money to pay all the necessary expenses and they had some other considerations delaying their departure. In the end, I received two pink exit visas with our photos. That day I took a train from Odesa to Belgorod-Dnestrovsky. We still had to pack for the journey to Israel. In these last few days before the new year of 1972, I wanted to spend time with my family.

With our exit visas, I ordered tickets to travel by train from Belgorod-Dnestrovky to Odesa on the morning of January 1, 1972, and on the same day, before lunchtime, from Odesa to Moscow. As well, I ordered a train ticket from Moscow to Vienna for January 3. After that was done, I went to the post office to call Mark Geizer to confirm that Hanna and I would be in Moscow on the afternoon of January 2. Mark gave me the address of his wife's mother and told me that she would accommodate us for one night.

My packing was quick and straightforward. I had only one small suitcase to take; I packed it with my math books, documents, and underwear. Hanna did her packing. My mother still worked at the fish factory, and almost every day she would bring home a few fresh fish. One day, my mom told us that many police officers inside and outside the factory caught people taking fish. My mom had become aware of this operation earlier in the day, so she didn't take fish home that afternoon. She saw a few workers being searched on the way from work and arrested. I begged my mom not to take fish from work from now on because this could severely jeopardize the possibility of their future emigration to Israel, or she could be arrested and imprisoned. My mom asked me to stop worrying about her as everything would be all right. I worried very much about my mom during the last days I spent at home.

My mom cooked a nice meal for New Year's Eve, and she invited our neighbor Assia, the mother of my friend Stanislav "Stas" Manovski, to join us.

We were five people at the table, Dad and Mom, Hanna and I, and Assia. As the evening progressed toward midnight, I asked Assia about her husband. I knew that he was supposed to be released from prison, but something had happened to him while I was away from home in Odesa. Assia confirmed that her husband had been released and had come home. Unfortunately, he had broken his leg and wasn't mobile. The police came for him again and took him to prison. He got another ten-year sentence. This time, Assia couldn't get an explanation from the police or the justice department, but she learned why her husband went to prison a second time when he told her shortly after his release.

He spent about fifteen years of his first sentence in a labor camp near Kuibyshev, now known as Samara, northeast of the Caspian Sea. He was a lead engineer in the construction of a large river dam and hydro station that would provide electricity to the region. Unfortunately, his sentence ended a few years before the project would, so government officials arrested him again and sent him back to work on the dam.

I cautiously asked her what kind of life her husband had led there away from his family for so many years. She was frank with us and told us that lead engineers had a certain degree of freedom within the construction zone and that, most likely, he had found another woman to look after him there to make his days a bit brighter. Many years later, visiting us in Toronto, Stas told me that he had a younger brother in Kuibyshev—one who looked very similar to him!

As the clock reached midnight, signaling the beginning of the new year 1972, I took two glasses of wine and a plate with some food and a few pieces of cake from the table and went outside, as I had done every year since returning from military services. One block from our apartment was an army warehouse in the basement of the city's hotel. This warehouse held military clothing and boots for soldiers. The warehouse was guarded twenty-four hours a day, seven days a week, by armed soldiers. In solidarity with soldiers standing on guard on New Year's Eve, I always took some wine and food to the warehouse. Usually, a soldier on guard would refuse to accept anything from me, as the military book of rules prohibited this. However, after I explained who I was and why I was bringing wine and food that night, the soldier would warm to the idea that he could also celebrate like a human being. On New Year's Eve 1972 the night was quite warm and I didn't wear a jacket or a coat; I was wearing a white shirt. I wished the soldier on guard a happy new year, army service with no hardship, and a speedy release. We drank our glasses of wine, he ate what I had put on the plate, and I returned home.

The next morning, four of us—Mom, Dad, Hanna, and I—took the train to Odesa. A few days earlier, I had called my comrades from the synagogue in Odesa to inform them that on January 1, I would be departing to Moscow, and then to Vienna. Many of them were waiting for us at the Odesa train station. When I saw a group of ten or fifteen people, I asked them not to make a party, demonstration, or noise, and not to attract the attention of the police as this could cause the police to prevent me from taking my trip. We hugged each other, and I collected information from some of my friends as to who needed invitations for emigration to Israel. The only legal way—at that time—to leave the Soviet Union was for family reunification. I was "lucky" to have three aunts in Israel, but many Jews in the Soviet Union didn't have relatives there. So, I had started collecting names and addresses of Jews who wanted to emigrate but had no relatives in Israel. I knew that there were organizations in Israel helping with invitations, even for those who technically had no Israeli relatives. In the last two months, I had written many names in my special notebook and promised these people to do my best to help them with the papers they needed.

We had about an hour between trains, and I filled a few more names into my "secret" notebook. While doing this, I noticed that Galina Kirova had also come to say goodbye to me. She was standing alone, away from the group, and she didn't make any signals to me and said nothing. She stood and watched my sister and I board the train to Moscow. I waved to her, but she didn't react, or didn't want to show her reaction, as she was probably aware of the undercover police and KGB there. I am not sure how she found out that I was departing from Odesa on that day and time, but she knew.

Hanna and I hugged and kissed our parents and took our place in the car going to Moscow. The car was packed and noisy, and we arrived in Moscow on the afternoon of January 2. It was very cold, almost −13°F. We took a taxi to Ostankino, an area in Moscow near the TV tower and All-Union Agricultural Exhibition Center. Mark Geizer's mother-in-law lived in an apartment on the second floor of an old, two-story multifamily building. A wooden balcony ran along the second floor, and doors to the flats opened to the balcony like in a motel. Hanna and I took the stairs to the second floor, found the apartment, and knocked on the door. Unfortunately, nobody was home yet. It was close to 5 p.m. and it was very, very cold outside.

My First Meeting with Fania

Ten minutes later, a beautiful young girl came to the same door, knocked on it, and looked around aimlessly and forlornly after figuring out that nobody was home yet. I asked her, "Are you also visiting someone in this apartment?"

"Yes."

I told her that we too were waiting for the owner, who should show up at any moment. "So, let us wait together," I offered. "Please join our company."

She held a zinc container with a lid; she was dressed a bit lightly, not for Moscow's winter, although she did have a warm shawl on her head. "Do you live in Moscow?" I asked her.

"No, I'm here on holiday. I'm visiting my relatives." She introduced herself: "My name is Fania."

We continued with light banter for ten or fifteen minutes until the apartment owner, Dora Efimovna Kotlyar, the mother of Mark Geizer's wife Mary, arrived from work. We were miserably cold, so she quickly ushered us into her apartment. Fania had caught my eye.

Dora Efimovna was a widow, as her husband had been accused by the Soviet courts of economic crime and sentenced to death in 1962. His crime was in exploiting the unsatisfactory production of cosmetics for Soviet women. Mr. Kotlyar and his friends, skillful entrepreneurs, acquired special equipment to produce women's lipstick and sold their products in many cities. Any entrepreneurial activities by private citizens were prohibited, as the Soviet government had an absolute monopoly on all production of goods. Mr. Kotlyar and his friends were arrested and, after a symbolic trial, Mr. Kotlyar was sentenced to death, although he wasn't the most important member of his team. He was a Jew. Later, I learned that Fania's father was sentenced to death in another famous "economic crime" trial, the Frunze Affair, in the city of Frunze (now Bishkek), the capital of the Soviet republic of Kyrgyzstan, in 1962.[2]

Although Dora Efimovna was quite bitter about losing her husband ten years earlier and generally in a sour mood, she was very hospitable. She asked Fania what she was doing in Moscow. Fania explained that she had come to Moscow from Frunze with a group of students for winter vacation. Her brother Roma was the vice principal of a school in Frunze, but he had fallen

---

2   The Frunze Affair is described in Chapter 6.

ill and sent Fania in his stead as chaperone. Fania took a half day off work to visit Dora Efimovna, a cousin of her mother, and brought Dora Efimovna a small gift from her mother: a container of beautiful apples (certainly a treat in Moscow during winter!) from Frunze.

While Dora Efimovna set a long table for supper, Mark and Mary arrived to meet with us. Soon after, a group of young men unknown to me also came to celebrate our departure to Israel. They brought a few bottles of vodka and a cake. As we sat down and started eating, Dora Efimovna filled our glasses with alcohol. We ate and drank, and our conversation started flowing freely, but quietly. Nobody wanted to disturb the neighbors.

I sat at one side of the long table, Fania at the other end. She was so attractive, with dark black hair and deep blue "Jewish eyes" (perhaps reflective of some kind of soulful, feminine Jewish wisdom), and yet she seemed so innocent and timid. She didn't talk much, didn't have conversations with anyone, and mostly sat, ate, and listened to what these big-city Moscow people were talking about.

Fania in Moscow, January 2, 1972.

I had a few shots of vodka, ate the delicious food Dora Efimovna had made, and finished half a jar of wild mushrooms she had marinated. Then I stood up to give a speech about why every "thinking" Jew in the Soviet Union must consider emigrating to Israel. I asked if anyone at the table needed help getting an invitation from a "relative" in Israel for family reunification. A few people in the room indicated they had such a need, so I pulled out my little notebook and asked them, one by one, to give me the information I required for such invitations. As I walked around the table, I approached Fania and asked her if she would like to go to Israel. Fania answered that she didn't know if she would like to leave her family. Then she admitted that she didn't know anything about Israel. In Frunze, far away from the European part of the Soviet Union, they didn't receive much information about Israel and were not aware that it was possible to emigrate.

I told her that I would be waiting to marry her if she decided to come to Israel. It was crazy of me to say such words—to offer marriage to the most innocent girl I ever met and one I had only known for hours—on my last evening in the Soviet Union. It was crazy of me to say these words at all! Of course, I was both very stressed and excited that I was leaving the country, and I had been drinking quite a lot of vodka to relax a bit. So, my mind was obviously not in its more rational state—but I asked Fania to give me her information for an invitation to Israel, and she could decide later if she wanted to join me in the Holy Land. I couldn't even imagine that this very special evening was a pivotal moment for me. I sealed my fate then in my book of life. Eventually, Fania joined me in Jerusalem (but not without significant obstacles, including imprisonment!) and we married shortly after her arrival. Fifty-something years later, we are very much in love.

The guests left late that evening, and six of us prepared for sleep. Dora Efimovna gave each of us a pillow and blankets; we slept on the floor till dawn. Early in the morning, Dora Efimovna left to go to work, Fania to be with her students. Mark and Mary prepared a small breakfast before Hanna and I took a bus to the Belorussky Railroad Terminal, the station for trains going to the Western part of the Soviet Union and Europe. The train we needed was long, but only a few cars would cross the border out of the Soviet Union. These were international cars serving foreign diplomats, journalists, tourists, and people with emigration visas like Hanna and myself.

After a few hugs with Mark and Mary, Hanna and I went up into our car and settled in our cabin. After I had spent many days in regular smelly train cars traveling between Moscow, Odesa, Kyiv, and Belgorod-Dnestrovsky, international cars were a different experience. They were not crowded, the passengers were quiet and considerate, and our cabin was spotless with white tablecloths, proper sleeping shelves, clean bedding, and a bottle of clean drinking water and flowers on the table.

The train departed half an hour after we settled into the cabin. Mark and Mary left a few minutes after we climbed into the car; we didn't see any familiar faces outside the windows when the train moved away. I had very ambivalent feelings: sad but happy in these final moments, leaving behind our miserable existence in this country that was supposed to be called our Motherland. I was finally released from the smothering hug of my Motherland, but I couldn't quite shake the feeling that I hadn't yet gotten away. I wished to sleep for the next twenty-four hours and simply awaken on the other side of the border, awake in the truly free world as a reborn man.

Escape to Israel

The train didn't move quickly, as it made frequent stops in small towns all the way to Chop, a small city in the Carpathian Mountains area near where the Soviet Union met Czechoslovakia (as it was then) and Hungary. There were no new passengers for international cars from these places; the new passengers were accommodated in regular Soviet cars.

Soviet railroads had a wider gauge than European ones, so Soviet trains couldn't travel on European railroads and European trains couldn't travel into the Soviet Union. Chop was a railroad depot for mounting European cars on Soviet platforms and Soviet cars on European platforms. I was warned that we might be ordered out of our car during this process, and then we might be searched one last time by Soviet customs and the KGB. Emigrants were prohibited from taking any of a long list of items out of the Soviet Union, including particular literature, certain photos, jewelry, money, documents, and more. Hanna and I had no items from this list in our two small suitcases; nonetheless, we could be searched.

As the train pulled up to the Chop station, an armed border guard, a soldier, and a few more men in civilian clothes entered our cabin and asked for our papers. Then they asked us to open our suitcases and quickly perused the contents. My suitcase was filled with my math books, underwear, family photos, and handwritten parts of my diploma thesis. Hanna's suitcase had similar. After about ten minutes of inspection, we were told not to leave the car while transferring to a European platform. This result—having a successful inspection and being permitted to remain in the car—was a relief to us.

We witnessed others who were not as fortunate. Some Jewish families had brought baggage with household items and personal belongings. The USSR sometimes permitted families to pack some of their belongings into large wooden boxes and send these to Israel on the same train they would travel in to Vienna. When a family with such boxed belongings would come to Chop, they had to take their boxes to customs inspection. If such a family had luck enough to receive their boxes at Chop (oftentimes these items would go missing), it would take them a few hours to complete the inspection and, if there were no problems, they would need to catch a train to Vienna the same day.

Many families arrived in Chop a day or two ahead of their baggage. They would be stranded for a few days, sleeping on the train station floor, as there were no hotels in Chop. Quite often, such families ran into problems with Soviet customs. Most of the customs officers were corrupt and expected a bribe to make their inspection relatively easier. Some people knew about this expectation and had a sizable amount of money or valuables to "oil" the process. But many others, mainly those from peripheral regions of the Soviet Union or older people, were subjected to long and humiliating customs searches of their baggage, and even body searches. These poor souls were stuck for days in Chop with nobody to help them and no authority to appeal to. Hanna and I were fortunate in this regard. We sat in our car, read books, and observed what was going on through our window.

More people joined us in our compartment in the night as the work of transferring cars onto platforms continued and cars going to other European destinations were added to the train. We finally left Chop the following afternoon and slowly crossed the border into Slovakia, then part of the Socialist Republic of Czechoslovakia. Some stress remained on my shoulders while we remained in a zone of Soviet influence and control. We were free, but not exactly free yet.

The train arrived in the Slovakian capital of Bratislava that evening. We were told that it would be there for a few hours as they needed to separate cars destined for Vienna from the train and attach new cars with passengers from Slovakia. As I started to prepare for a night of rest, a few young Georgians came to our compartment and begged for help. While in Chop, some Georgian Jewish families were put into the wrong cars, ones not destined for Vienna. These families had many kids, older people, and lots of luggage. They needed to be relocated into our car, and they needed strong hands to help them with their belongings. There were no Slovakian workers in the station to help us or provide us with dollies or other equipment. Along with several other young guys from our car, I jumped out and ran to the end of the long train to rescue these poor people. I ran up to the last car, grabbed two suitcases that belonged to those who needed help, ran with these to my car, left them there, and ran back again for more. One of the family members we were helping stayed in our car and distributed the luggage we were bringing into particular cabins. We ran back and forth with heavy luggage while some women walked their children and the elderly to our car. We moved lots of baggage—and it was tough work.

As I ran back to my car on my last run, I realized that the front half of our train had detached from the back portion and already moved away. I looked around and couldn't see the train with my compartment and Hanna. The train station was very large, with many lines used to assemble cars into a train. Two Slovakian guys were doing some work in the midst of lines running in different directions. I asked them which train was going to Vienna. Although the Slovakian language is Slavic, they could hardly understand what I was asking, but after a few minutes, they understood that I was lost and showed me the direction I needed to go. It was way after midnight and very foggy. As I was running, I heard Hanna's voice yelling, "Roma, where are you?" The train was still moving slowly when I saw Hanna standing at the door of our compartment, crying. I ran as fast as I could and jumped onto the stairs of the compartment, with the train moving as I walked inside. I was exhausted, terrified by the prospect of almost missing my train to freedom, and quite happy to continue our journey to Vienna.

The train arrived in Vienna in the early morning. There were no other trains and no other people on the platform except for a few heavily armed Austrian police officers with bulletproof jackets and machine guns. Few civilians came up to our train and nobody came to our compartment or waved to us. As passengers stepped out onto the station's platform, the civilians who did come to meet us introduced themselves as representatives of the Jewish Agency for Israel (HaSochnut haYehudit l'Eretz Yisrael), an organization whose responsibilities included immigration and absorbing immigrants in Israel. In broken Russian, they asked each of us in our train compartment if any person's or family's destination was Israel. Those who said no were directed to another group of officials, representatives of Jewish Immigrant

Aid Services (JIAS), and taken to a room in the station. Those of us who confirmed that we were headed to Israel were taken to buses waiting outside.

Before we left, I asked a Jewish Agency representative about my "secret notebook" with the names and contact information of people in the Soviet Union who needed an invitation for immigration to Israel—to whom should I provide my notebook? The Agency representative called another Israeli representative who seemed to be the correct person for this task, and I handed it to him.

From there, many buses took us to Schönau Castle outside Vienna—there were perhaps 200 people with us leaving the Soviet Union and heading for Israel. As our bus traveled along the streets of Vienna, we were glued to the window, mystified by the clean streets and walkways, the famous Austrian architecture, and the beautiful little storefronts and cafés. It was still morning and there were not many people outside, but everything appeared so magically organized and immaculate. I felt that even the air we were breathing that morning was the air of freedom and was full of anticipation of a new life.

As the bus took us to Schönau Castle, we asked the Jewish Agency chaperone why there were no people on the platform at the train station upon our arrival except for a few heavily armed policemen. Their explanation was that Palestinian Arabs were not happy with the growing emigration of Soviet Jews to Israel and trying to sabotage this emigration with acts of terror. That was why our train's arrival was scheduled for early morning, when armed police could easily keep the train's platform free from other people. That is also why the bus was taking us to Schönau Castle, outside Vienna, as the police could organize security forces and processes to prevent any terror attacks. Such measures had been introduced after a few recent terrorist acts. After these unfortunate events, the Jewish Agency had leased Schönau Castle and used it for emigration services instead of the hotel in Vienna that they had previously used, which was an easy target.

Schönau Castle was near a quaint Austrian village. It had a few large, auditorium-like halls on the main floor and a few small rooms organized as offices. The halls were filled with many beds to accommodate single people; families with young children were accommodated in smaller spaces on upper floors. We were told that we were going to stay two or three days before an El Al flight took us to Israel. Hanna and I settled in and we made a few new friends.

On the second day, a man came from the Israeli consulate in Vienna and called my name. He took me to one of the offices and presented himself, in broken Russian, as a consular official responsible for Russian immigrants to Israel. He pulled my notebook from his pocket and asked me to explain how I collected people's information. He asked questions about these people, listened carefully, and made notes in his papers. It took a few hours to explain the details of my participation in Odesa's Jewish movement for emigration, my studies at the university, my military service in the Red Army, and my mother's visit to Israel during the Six Day War. When we finished, he opened a safety box built into the wall in this room and pulled out a bottle of cognac and two glasses. He poured a shot for himself and filled up my glass. We made a L'Chaim. He thanked me for all that I had done and for the information I had passed along to him. He also said he was certain that I would settle nicely in Israel and be taken good care of upon arrival at Lod Airport, but I didn't pay much attention to his words at the time.

The same afternoon, a young guy from Soviet Georgia invited a few of us to the bar in the village beside Schönau Castle. I told him that I had no money, but he pulled a pack of American dollars out of his pocket and said he would pay. Curious about how he had avoided the many searches by customs and police, I asked him how he had managed to smuggle such a large amount of money out of the USSR. With a laugh, he said that money could buy everything in the USSR, and he knew how and whom to bribe. Then he pulled a small velvet bag from another pocket and showed us a few sparkling diamonds. He said that he and his family had risked their lives making good money in Georgia by growing citrus fruits and selling them in much colder parts of the Soviet Union. They were determined to bring their wealth with them to Israel. Now he wanted a small celebration with us in the village. We got the okay from the Israeli authorities in the castle and went to the bar. The others ordered vodka, whiskey, and cognac, but I stupidly ordered Coca-Cola, expecting it to be beer. After taking a sip, I realized that this was a strange-tasting nonalcoholic drink. The taste was very artificial. I wouldn't say I liked it then, and I never developed a liking for it later.

We were told that our flight to Israel was scheduled for the evening of our third day in Schönau Castle. In the late afternoon, we boarded buses and were taken to Vienna Airport. Again, the buses had to cross the city, and we were once again transfixed, staring out of the bus windows. As our bus passed through the streets in the city center, we were in awe of the gleaming store windows. The lighting stores and furniture stores were especially riveting, as was the famous Vienna Opera House. Several hours at the airport passed before we boarded the El Al airplane. Again, we saw many Austrian armed police officers patrolling the area where we were waiting to be processed and the boarding area. The plane departed after midnight to arrive in Israel early in the morning. I felt enormous trepidation and anticipation. I was about to enter the unknown; that said, I was full of hope.

CHAPTER 6

Beyond Soviet Borders

_____

Israel

Memories of my first days in Israel are still fresh in my mind. The plane landed at Lod Airport (now Ben Gurion). From a large waiting room in the terminal, we were called individually to be processed by immigration officers. When I was called, the immigration officer asked for my papers. He asked if I had a Jewish first name. I told him that I was given the name Riven when I was born, but I changed it to Roman to avoid antisemitic attacks and discrimination in the USSR. He looked at me, said my Hebrew name should be Reuven, and wrote that in his papers.

When he asked me what my plans were for my new life in Israel, I told him that I had served in the Red Army and was a qualified army officer in military communications for short- and mid-range distances and I was ready to join the Israeli army. The officer laughed and told me that I needed to learn Hebrew first and understand life in Israel before joining the army. That would take time, so I had to start learning the language soon. He said that he had received good references about me from the Israeli consulate in Vienna; their recommendation was to send me to Ulpan Etzion in Jerusalem (an _ulpan_ is a school where newcomers learn Hebrew). The officer asked me if any of my Israeli family were meeting me at the airport. I answered that I wasn't sure since I hadn't yet communicated with them. The officer laughed again and told me not to worry; someone was waiting for me outside. I received a newcomer certificate (_Teudat Oleh_) and other papers and came out to wait for Hanna. She came out from another room with her documents in hand; she had also been assigned to Ulpan Etzion. Later, when we arrived at the ulpan, I understood that both of us truly had been taken good care of by the Vienna consulate.

Aunt Zipora (my mom's eldest sister) and her husband Haim met us outside—quite worried because it had taken us so long in immigration.

After a half-hour ride, we arrived at their home, a second-floor apartment adjacent to a small park in Petah Tikva. It was still morning; there was lots of sunshine in the apartment. After Zipora opened the windows, the fresh air and the scent of flowers from the bushes below the windows and the sounds of various birds filled the apartment. I was in heaven; I was drunk with everything I experienced and saw that day. We had breakfast with grapefruit, oranges, juices, omelet, and sweet buns with hot cocoa.

Aunt Zipora and Haim had left Bessarabia in 1929 and mainly spoke Hebrew and Yiddish; nonetheless, they did speak Russian—mixed with Yiddish—and we could communicate, however poorly. They asked many questions about my mom and dad and our lives in the USSR. They took me by the hand and walked me around their apartment to show me their TV set, fridge and stove, and other household items (assuming that I had never seen these items). Certainly, we didn't have most of the items in our home; they were, however, available either in the stores or on the black markets—people could buy them if they had enough money. I was surprised that they thought that Hanna and I came from a completely impoverished Third World country and felt a twinge of insult; however, I realized that we were their guests and, out of respect for their age and hospitality, I stopped explaining that I was pretty familiar with many of the things they proudly showed us.

Their two sons, Yehoshua and Reuven, came by after the workday to see us. The eldest, Yehoshua, lost his left arm in one of the wars between Israel and the Arab countries; the younger, Reuven, lost his right hand handling equipment in their family business. The two of them ran a large laundromat serving restaurants and hotels in Tel Aviv. Zipora and Haim had a dry cleaner's shop in Petah Tikva, near the city's marketplace. All of them were well established. While drinking coffee with Zipora's cookies and cake, my cousins tried to talk to us, but we didn't know Hebrew. They switched to Yiddish, but we were also very weak in that language. Zipora and Haim tried to be translators to help us, but this didn't go well. Before my cousins went home, Reuven told us, through Zipora, that tomorrow morning he and his wife Rivka would come to pick us up to go to Tel Aviv, about thirty minutes away.

They took us to Dizengoff Street in the center of Tel Aviv, which was full of small retailers' shops, coffee shops with tables outside, and stands selling falafel, magazines, and newspapers. Since I had never heard of pizza, Reuven took us to a pizza stand, bought us each a large slice, and explained—in Yiddish—that Italian food had become fashionable in Israel. After that, Rivka took us to a large department store to buy some clothes. After looking at my old Soviet pants, she commented that, since I would be studying in the ulpan in Jerusalem, I needed to improve my wardrobe.

She told us that Ulpan Etzion was specifically intended for well-educated youth from the United States, Australia, France, England, Canada, and other Western countries. She insisted that without better clothing we would look poor and strange compared to the other students. She took me to the rack with men's suits and asked me to choose whatever I wanted. I wasn't experienced in buying suits, so I chose one made of light brown corduroy (something modern) and another one that was simpler in style. After trying these on, I continued walking along Dizengoff, wearing my new corduroy suit. Rivka also bought a few dresses for Hanna.

The next morning, Haim and Zipora took us to Ulpan Etzion in Jerusalem. After a short registration procedure, they left for home in Petah Tikva while Hanna and I settled in the ulpan's dormitory. Hanna was accommodated in a dorm room with three other girls; I got a room with three other guys. Everything felt great; I was ready for my first Hebrew class the next day. There was lunch and supper served in the dining room in the ulpan. It was there that I ate my first real Israeli meal; it was so full of flavor from Middle Eastern spices and vegetables that I had never encountered in the Soviet Union. I took a stroll to learn about my surroundings and arrived at the old train station. A road continued steeply down into a narrow valley, then went up to the Old City walls. The scenery was breathtaking.

Hanna and I joined the class the next day. There were about ten students, all between the ages of twenty and thirty, all from different countries, all with university degrees, and all eager to start learning Hebrew. The teacher—a Jewish woman who had immigrated to Israel from Bulgaria as a child—knew how to manage a class with students who could communicate neither with her nor with one another. She taught us a few essential words, the Hebrew alphabet (and the use of dots above, below, and in front of Hebrew letters), and perspectives on Judaism and Israel: Jewish holidays, traditions, and a bit of the Torah. Because I was aching to discover my heritage, I was able to learn the basics quickly. Basic Hebrew was very structural and, with my background in math, I easily understood how to build nouns, verbs, and adjectives from three-letter roots. In two months, I had sufficient vocabulary to handle simple conversation and read magazines written using fairly basic Hebrew.

One day, I received a phone call from one of the Jewish Agency (Sochnut) offices regarding invitations for emigration to Israel for the people I had listed in my black book. I was told that I could send them messages or letters to expect those invitations. I started writing letters to every person in my small black book telling them that their relatives in Israel were very happy for the opportunity to see them in Israel and that they could soon expect official papers for family reunification. Some of the people I wrote to responded with gratitude, and some didn't respond.

On a seemingly uneventful evening, a middle-aged man with red curly hair and a brown leather jacket came to the Ulpan's dormitory and asked if somebody there was from Odesa. The dormitory guard pointed at me. The man presented himself as a representative of the Labour (Avoda) Party. He was assigned the duty of helping with the absorption/integration of newcomers from the Soviet Union. He spoke Russian with a slight accent and said that his parents were from Odesa; after a short chat, he offered Hanna and me a ride in his car to show us Jerusalem. He continued to visit me in the Ulpan every week or two. On one occasion, he offered a small amount of money as a loan from his party and the Histadrut (Workers Union). I declined the offer, but Hanna took the money as she was more pragmatic. He came to the ulpan and asked me to dress in nice clothes, since he was taking me to the Israeli president's residence. The residency was not far from the Jerusalem Theater. A large group of people were gathered in the auditorium, expecting President Zalman Shazar, his wife, and a few ministers. I still remember one of the ministers there, Uzi Narkiss, a minister responsible for the absorption of immigrants. After a few speeches, which I hardly understood, I was presented to the president.

Reuven shaking hands with Israeli President Zalman Shazar, 1972.

The evening was very memorable. However, a few days afterwards, our patron came to the Ulpan again and called Hanna and me into an empty classroom. He said that he wished to make our absorption into Israel easy and to provide us with a platform for a successful life. He complimented us and flattered us for our bravery and good education. It all seemed rather excessive. And he finished by saying that it was the proper time for us to accept his advice to become members of Avoda and sign up to become part of the Histadrut. He told us that we would be protected and our memberships would open doors to a better life, better jobs, and better social opportunities. His speech reminded me of all the perks people received when they became members of the Communist Party in the USSR, the key positions at work and so forth that they enjoyed in exchange for acting as KGB informers. I understood that our patron was on a "fishing expedition." His actual assignment was the recruitment of recent immigrants from the Soviet Union into the Labour Party. My answer to him that day was that I had left the Soviet Union because I hated the Communist Party, government corruption, corruption at places of work, and, overall, any "isms." My Soviet experience was still too fresh, and I was not able to accept his offer. I apologized profusely. After about an hour of going back and forth trying to change my mind, the guy left frustrated and I never saw him again.

Not too long after avoiding political recruitment I had a pleasant surprise; I received a letter from Fania Shtramvasser from Frunze, Kyrgyzstan. She wrote that she was eager to join me after she got the invitation papers. She asked me to write about my life in Israel, about the ulpan, and other things. We started exchanging letters every month. I had to be careful about what and how I wrote to Fania; I knew that all our letters were opened and read by the KGB. Our long-distance relationship grew warmer with every letter, and I realized that our first short meeting on my last day in Moscow wasn't a chance event. What I didn't anticipate was how terrible Fania's life (and the lives of her family members) would become because of our contact.

At the end of March, I received a request to visit the security services office in Tel Aviv regarding my time in the Red Army. On my way there, I stopped in Petah Tikva to meet Mike (Misha) Barenboim, the brother of my first-year university classmate Grisha (Gregory) Barenboim. Before leaving Odesa for Moscow, Gregory called me and gave me the contact information of his brother Misha, who had left for Israel with his family a year before me. While in the ulpan, I contacted him and visited him and his family in Petah Tikva. Misha was a talented engineer with a master's degree from the Odesa Polytechnic Institute. He already had an engineering job, and his family had purchased an apartment. We met a few hours before my appointment time in Tel Aviv.

I talked to Misha about my hesitancy to share my knowledge and experiences in the Red Army with the Israeli security agents. Good or bad, I had taken an oath not to divulge any information about military service in the Soviet Union during my service nor after my release into civilian life. I had sworn the oath in 1964, when I was drafted into the army, but many things had happened between then and 1972, and I needed some advice to clear my mind. Misha was smart, and I hoped that he could understand my ambivalence. That day, he was home in the morning, and he was happy to talk with me. I told him what was on my mind: On the one hand, I was Israeli now, and I had obligations to my new and real home, but on the other, I was still under oath to the Red Army. I needed to choose what to do at the security meeting that day.

After we talked back and forth for about half an hour, Misha asked me a few questions that quickly cleared my mind. He asked me about life in the Soviet Union. Did the Soviet government provide jobs with sufficient income for my parents while they had to work long hours of backbreaking labor? What had happened at my entrance exams to Moscow University? Had I been accepted into the PhD program at Odesa University? Why was it okay for me to write a PhD thesis for someone else but not for myself? How easy was it for me to find a job after completing my master's degree? Even though the Soviet constitution declared that every citizen had equal rights, did the Soviet government uphold my rights as a Jew? The last question removed all my hesitations: if the Soviet constitution was a big lie and life in the USSR was full of antisemitism, why should I feel that I was still under oath to them?

I was well-received in Tel Aviv, and I spent a few hours discussing my life in the USSR in general terms, my military service in greater detail. Two Israeli agents were particularly interested in the events around the Six Day War and the American spy plane downed in the Black Sea. At the end of the meeting, they asked me to return in two weeks to share my stories with more people.

When I arrived at the same office two weeks later, five men were waiting for me: the same two Israeli men and three officers in American Air Force uniforms. These three officers spoke English, and one of them spoke Russian with a heavy accent. The second conversation focused on the airbase in Sevastopol, where I had spent two and a half years. The Americans asked me about the plane that had been downed in the Black Sea; they wanted to know what we did to the plane's wing while it was on our runway. I was then asked about the training flights: How were they scheduled, where did our pilots typically fly, and how had we prepared for flights? It was about five years since I had left the army, and I had completely forgotten that, an hour before training flights, one small MiG 17 jet would fly to the training zone to check meteorological and ground conditions; the actual training flights wouldn't begin until the return of that preliminary flight. Indeed, I had prepared many of these reconnaissance flights, but at that moment, in front of five men, my mind went blank. On the bus back to Jerusalem, I suddenly realized that I had forgotten such an important fact—and I worried that they may not have trusted my stories, simply because of my memory lapse.

After Passover 1972, in April, I realized that our studies in the ulpan would be over very soon, and I had to prepare for my future. My main goal was to earn a PhD from the Hebrew University, a degree that had been denied me in my past reality. My backup plan was to look for any employment my education could allow. That was easy: I took my master's thesis, made copies of my university diploma and the marks that I had earned in all major subjects, went to the Hebrew University's admissions office at the Givat Ram campus, and submitted my application. I was told that an answer should come in two weeks.

At the beginning of May I received an invitation from the Hebrew University to meet with some officials and math professors. When I arrived, I was congratulated by the university registrar for being accepted into a PhD program. I was told that the evaluation committee had confirmed my degree and had given a very favorable review of my master's thesis. My master's thesis was about 85 percent of a completed doctoral thesis project; however, to earn my PhD I would need to complete some mandatory courses and work under the mentorship and supervision of a Hebrew University professor. This was similar to what was expected from all doctoral students in the Soviet Union. In Israel, fortunately, the one exception was that the course on the history and philosophy of the Communist Party wasn't needed! So far, everything I heard in the office was encouraging and inspiring.

They then sent me to the math and physics building to meet with Professor S. Agmon. I hadn't done my homework, so I didn't know anything about him at that meeting. He was working in his office when I arrived. We had a long conversation: he asked me a lot about Odesa University, Mark Krein's seminars, and my master's thesis. He admitted that he had checked my results in the master's thesis; however, he had been unable to decide on the value of my work because he wasn't an expert on theories of stability of ordinary differential equations. He told me that he had accepted me into the PhD program under his supervision and mentorship because his field of expertise, functional analysis, was the closest among all professors at the Hebrew University to my field in differential equations. He was unsure how he would help me complete my research and turn my master's thesis into a PhD dissertation, but he would give me some leads at Tel Aviv University and Haifa's Technion at a later date.

At the end of our first meeting, Professor Agmon asked me if my family was in Israel and if I had a source of income. When he heard my negative answers, he asked me to go back to the office to meet with some clerks there. After a quick call to ensure that his information was up to date, he told me that the university was looking for a Russian-speaking mathematician willing to teach first-year students. He sent me to the office, where they asked me if I would undertake an assistant professorship: I would be providing lectures to large classes (fifty-plus students in each). They told me that many students had registered for the school year beginning in October 1972. These students were not native Israelis, and the university intended to offer them an education in their native languages (English, French, Spanish, and Russian). There would be some freedom in course planning, and I would be given a syllabus and teaching materials. I would have to build lesson plans, practicum, and tutorials for Russian immigrant students. At the end of the year, all teaching staff would create a common exam for all groups, translate this exam into the native languages of their students, run the written exam, and mark the results. These courses would be delivered at Mount Scopus, an older campus. Because I would be a PhD student, teaching would be my part-time job, and I would receive good pay for a few hours' teaching. The deal was sealed by a six-month contract that could be extended for another six months, pending my good performance. I was delighted by this opportunity and signed my first contract on the spot.

My teaching job at the university was to start at the end of September, while my studies at Ulpan Etzion finished in mid-May. I felt that my Hebrew was still weak, and I wanted to fill my summer learning Hebrew to communicate better at the university, with my relatives, and on the streets. In my last days at the ulpan, I was invited to the office to discuss where I would settle in Israel. After hearing that I was accepted into a PhD program at the Hebrew University, I was offered accommodation—one room in a three-bedroom apartment for bachelors on Shtern Street in the Kiriat Yovel area of Jerusalem. My sister Hanna got accommodation in the city of Netanya. She relocated there, and I stayed in Jerusalem. I also discussed my desire to learn more Hebrew during the summer with the administrative office at the Ulpan. I asked if it would be possible for me to work at a summer camp for kids so that I could learn more Hebrew there. They asked me to call them at the beginning of June to see if they could help me out.

I was free for the summer. Every day, I spent a few hours reading newspapers in simple Hebrew, but I wanted to talk with Israelis to learn the spoken language better and obtain a deeper understanding of my new country. Fortunately, I received a message from the ulpan that they found me a job in a summer camp not far from Kiriat Yovel and provided me with contacts there. This particular camp was for kids from underprivileged families and was fully subsidized by the government. At the lowest point of the valley between Kiriat Yovel and another area were barracks that had been built about twenty-five years earlier to accommodate Jewish immigrants from Morocco. Many of these immigrants had little education or professions that were in demand in Israel, and had large families. Poverty was no stranger there.

I also met a few times with Professor Agmon. He introduced me to another doctoral student under his supervision—Russian-speaking Ilya (Eliyahu) Rips.[1] Ilya was younger than me by three years, looked very introverted and shy, and, honestly, I found him to be a bit strange. For one thing, he wore a knit hat on his head. Eventually, I learned that he wore the hat to cover burns that he had received to his body and head (self-immolation) during a 1969 protest against the Soviet invasion of Czechoslovakia—for which he spent two years in prison. Before his imprisonment, Ilya had been a very talented math student, was on the team representing the USSR in the Math Olympics, and had been accepted to university at fifteen years of age. I tried to build a friendly relationship with Ilya during our first year as PhD students, but it was tough because Ilya was seemingly very aloof and self-absorbed. I liked his honesty and mathematical talent, but it was hard to have

---

1 Rips later became quite famous as an Israeli mathematician of Latvian origin; he won various awards and became known for his research in geometric group theory. But that's not all - he became famous to the general public following his co-authoring a paper on what is popularly known as Bible Code, the supposed coded messaging in the Hebrew text of the Torah. Journalist Michael Drosnin wrote a best-sellling book (it reached No. 3 on *The New York Times's* non-fiction best-seller list) on Ilya's findings—The Bible Code— and even ended up on *The Oprah Winfrey Show* in 1997! The movie rights were sold to Warner Bros. (although the film was never produced). https://en.wikipedia.org/wiki/Eliyahu_Rips; https://www.imdb.com/title/tt12609864/.

a long conversation with him. Professor Agmon had a visible affinity to Ilya and spent more time mentoring him than me. Yes, I was a bit jealous then, but I knew in my heart that Ilya was on a higher level of talent in math than I was. I respected that, and I let Ilya know about it. We both received yearly plans for running and participating in math seminars for graduate and doctoral students.

In October, I started teaching students at the Mount Scopus campus. I enjoyed my class immensely. The students were mature and willing to work hard. I built a comprehensive and challenging program for which I was criticized by my colleagues teaching in other languages. They created coursework that was easier to match similar programs in their countries of origin. I had to explain to other teachers that, despite lots of difficulties in the Soviet Union, the math and physics education was superior for average and above-average students. I tried to argue that the best way to make students understand the material is to practice, and I offered a bet that my students would show better knowledge and results at the end of the course than my colleagues' students. I taught for three hours a week and spent another two hours in my practicum with my students. At every lesson, I reminded my students how important it was for them to do their homework on all of the topics we learned and offered them individual help if needed.

After getting paid the first time for my work at the university, I realized that it wasn't enough to cover my monthly needs. I also reviewed my contract with the university and realized that this was a short-term contract that would expire every six months—so I would have to renegotiate a new contract twice a year. In short, I needed an additional source of income. So, I decided to approach the Ministry of Education to inquire about a teaching position in one or more of Jerusalem's schools. The man with whom I eventually spoke was sympathetic to my immigration story, my acceptance to a doctoral program at the Hebrew University, and my teaching at the Mount Scopus campus. He told me that it was tough to find a vacant position for a teacher after the new school year had already begun; however, he had heard that one of the schools in Katamon might need a teacher. He called that school and, after speaking with the principal, he gave me a short reference letter and the school's address. He said that the principal there was waiting for me right away.

I arrived within half an hour. The school was within walking distance of Jerusalem's Theater and the Presidential Palace. At the time, Katamon had a reputation of being a not-so-safe neighborhood; however, I didn't know that at first. The principal, Dr. Kirshenbaum, received me in his office. After a short conversation, he looked into my eyes and asked how I would teach math if my Hebrew was so rudimentary and my accent was so Russian-heavy? I tried to explain to him that my language skills wouldn't be a barrier to teaching math. I was learning Hebrew quickly, and I promised him that he would see the results of my teaching very soon. He was very hesitant; I could see him thinking hard, looking at me, and then looking out the window behind his chair. In the end, he accepted me as a math teacher on probation: after all, I was a doctoral student and was working at the Hebrew University, I was young and energetic, and ultimately, he desperately needed a part-time math teacher!

He gave me four classes at different ends of the spectrum: two seventh-grade classes with excellent students and two classes with underprivileged kids. In Israel at that time, students were streamed based on their academic abilities. There were six seventh-grade classes. On one hand, the students in my first two classes were very advanced and were destined for university. On the other, the students in my other two classes were from families who were mostly Moroccan Jews, low-income, still living in the barracks, and poorly educated. In short, these kids—who were perhaps unfairly destined to learn trades, regardless of their natural abilities—needed special attention and I was committed to helping them get caught up and exceed expectations. They were equipped with simplified math books, and I noted that their curriculum was very different from the one I used in my first two classes. I was well received by the other teachers, particularly by my math vice-principal Michal Orev. She helped me understand how (and how not) to deal with students, parents, and the math programs. I was the youngest among the teachers, and they treated me like their child.

When I was next called into the office, Dr. Kirshenbaum told me of his desire to turn his school into one of the most desirable schools in Jerusalem. There were a few first-class junior high and high schools in exclusive city areas. The school in Katamon was not considered top-tier because of the unfortunate negative stereotypes attributed to the community of Jews—namely, Jews from Arab countries—who lived in the area. Dr. Kirshenbaum wanted to change this image by talking to professors at the Hebrew University and the offices of various government ministries in Jerusalem, asking them to send their kids or grandkids to his school and promising them an outstanding level of education—that he would create. The students in my higher-level classes were placed there because of their exceptionally high IQs. After having observed my work ethic and recognized my potential as a math teacher, Dr. Kirshenbaum offered me an extra responsibility—to create a unique and special after-school math program for super-talented students. He was straight with me: He wasn't an expert in math, but he trusted me and gave me carte blanche to create a high-level program. I was astonished and flattered by his words—but I realized how much work it would take and how much risk there would be. I was young and a bit naïve; I overestimated myself, and I took his offer.

Fania

From time to time, I bought a Russian-language Israeli newspaper to keep informed about immigration from the Soviet Union and the absorption of newcomers. I read articles about Jewish dissidents in Moscow, Leningrad, and other large cities in the Soviet Union to check if I would see any familiar names. One day, I noticed an article about the mass arrest of about seventy Jews in Moscow's Soviet Supreme Court. I read the names of the arrested people and, suddenly, I saw Fania Shtramvasser on the list! Since my time at the ulpan, I had sent her a few letters encouraging her to come to Israel. I was surprised to see her name among the names of people arrested in Moscow. I knew that she had applied for emigration and that her application had been refused. I assumed she traveled to Moscow to complain about the refusal of Frunze's police and the local KGB to grant her an exit visa. She had probably contacted some Moscow Jewish dissidents and was invited to submit her complaint to the Soviet Supreme Court with many other dissidents. That was the only logical explanation for her being arrested in Moscow.

With a borrowed typewriter and my slow typing, I wrote fiery letters to the KGB in Frunze and the Soviet Supreme Court, requesting that they let Fania come to Israel because I was waiting for her as my bride. I emphasized their inhumane policy of keeping people as prisoners in the Soviet Union while publicly presenting their constitution (that ostensibly guarantees fundamental human rights) to the West. At the end of my letters, I promised the KGB officials that I would go to New York and demonstrate in front of the United Nations building against the Soviet Union's treatment of Jews, particularly Fania. I had much inspiration to write these words, and it was easy for me to do so because I was already on the other side of the Iron Curtain—and free.

In the 1970s, more Jews began applying for permission to emigrate to Israel. Fania had applied in 1972 but was refused an exit visa by the Soviet authorities in Frunze. As I suspected, she then had traveled to Moscow and, on December 5, 1972—the Day of the Soviet Constitution—she went to the Soviet Supreme Court to apply for permission to emigrate. There, she joined a big group of Jewish people (over seventy others) petitioning for exit visas to Israel—an event organized by Ida Nudel (the famous activist known as the Guardian Angel or Angel of Mercy for her efforts to support refuseniks). The Soviet police had arrested all of the petitioners.

A month or so later—after I had nearly pulled my hair out writing letters, contacting the press and the UN, and cursing the KGB—I received a letter from Fania telling me that she was okay, at home in Frunze. She informed me that she wasn't working any more since she had returned home from Moscow after being arrested. Nobody would hire her and her previous workplace had dismissed her. Moreover, the KGB had warned her that they were soon going to send her to Siberia for a lifetime of labor since she wasn't working (but we both knew this catch-22: they were blocking her ability to work). Fania's older brother Roma also lost his job; his family was in great peril. The oldest brother, Iossif, who was a professor of math at South Ural Polytechnic Institute in the city of Cheliabinsk, feared for himself and his family. I understood that, without a doubt, she was now under KGB surveillance, and so was her family.

I wrote another bunch of angry letters to Frunze's KGB requesting Fania's release and I contacted the United Nations as well. I became deeply involved in helping Fania; we even talked on the phone once or twice at the beginning of 1973, even though we knew that we were being tracked and listened to. I felt terrible for her family; I could only imagine how upset they were. She and the other arrested petitioners were eventually called in for conversations with local authorities. After their interrogations, they were all—including Fania—loaded onto prison buses and sent to the notorious Lubyanka prison.[2]

---

2 Lubyanka prison has the reputation of being one of the most terrible prisons in history, known for its inhumane violence and torture (and often execution) of inmates. Many famous persons such as Aleksandr Solzhenitsyn and Raoul Wallenberg were interred there. For Russians, the word Lubyanka sounds as menacing as the word Gulag. In Soviet Russian jokes, Lubyanka was referred to as "the tallest building in Moscow", since Siberia (a euphemism for the Gulag labour camp system) could be "seen" from its basement. The prison was on the top floor, but since there were no windows on that floor, most prisoners, and therefore popular conception, thought they were being detained in its basement.

Fania was terrified to be in prison. Later, I would learn that she was initially placed in a cell with prostitutes and women who had committed violent crimes. She was barely twenty years old and quite reasonably afraid. To her credit, she demanded to be placed in solitary confinement, where she believed that she would be safer but had to wash the prison floors and complete other distasteful tasks. The prison guards gladly provided her that "comfort" assuming it would be an even bigger punishment for this refusenik, but being in prison with Ida Nudel and part of a large group of Jewish petitioners was actually a stroke of luck that helped Fania get an early release. Ida, however, had a difficult time of it and was sent to Siberia, only to be granted permission to leave the USSR at a much later date.

On April 24, 1973, a mailman came to my class's door during a lesson and delivered a short telegram from the Jewish Agency: Fania would arrive the next day on a flight from Vienna. Since I hadn't heard from Fania for a month, I was shocked. I realized that I wasn't emotionally prepared to meet her. Our only meeting, in Moscow, seemed like a dream from another reality; even our letters and my involvement in her release from prison seemed disconnected from the life I had been making for myself in Israel. I realized my promise of marriage was suddenly about to be put to the test. I asked for the next day off of school, ensured I had nothing scheduled for that day at the university, and took a bus to the airport to await Fania's arrival. I was told to wait for her outside the building.

Fania came out more than two hours after the plane from Austria landed and, at first, I didn't recognize her. She looked very different from the way I saw her in Moscow more than a year and a half ago. She was very thin and frail, dressed in a yellow dress, and obviously tired. She appeared so lost. Nevertheless, we were happy to see each other. I called a taxi and, as we left from the airport, I asked Fania where the Jewish Agency representatives at the airport had sent her. She answered that she didn't know, but maybe it was written in the papers she received. I looked at the Jewish Agency's forms and saw that they had directed Fania to her groom, Reuven Rashkovsky, in

---

While Lubyanka's most extreme dark history was more so in the past when Fania was held there, the ghosts of its terrible former times no doubt frightened anyone who did time in this prison (of course, one cannot understate that it was still no picnic to be a young, female dissident - thousands of kilometers from home - held there by the KGB in the 1970s). See: https://historycollection.com/18-inhumane-and-notorious-prisons-in-history/ and https://www.latimes.com/archives/la-xpm-1991-09-07-mn-1571-story.html.

Jerusalem. I asked Fania if the Jewish Agency representative had mentioned any ulpan where she could learn Hebrew, but he hadn't done so.

I was shocked that the Jewish Agency people never asked me if I had proper accommodations and the ability to take adequate care of Fania. I realized that I had no choice: I had to handle the situation, so I would accommodate Fania in my apartment. She was exhausted and sad, and I felt pity for her. When I asked her what she would like to eat first when we came home, she said she wanted oranges. Fortunately, I had plenty of oranges in my room, and I had some food in the fridge. We were alone in the apartment when we arrived. I gave Fania a few oranges after she took a shower, and I prepared a small meal. While we were eating, I made a plan for the night. I gave Fania my bed and put some stuff on the floor for myself. I introduced Fania to my neighbors when they came home and, after a short chat with them, she fell asleep on my bed (an Agency mattress filled with hay).

The next morning, I had to go to work. Fania didn't want to be alone in the apartment and asked me to take her with me to the school. I introduced Fania to Hannah Ratner, who worked in the chemistry lab, and left her with Hannah while I was teaching. I took Fania to the school's backyard during recesses to show her how Israeli kids played outside. As we were walking there, a boy from my lower-level class came from behind, slapped me on my shoulder and asked loudly, "Teacher, are you with another girl today?" Luckily, Fania didn't understand the Hebrew question, but she was shocked at the kid's inappropriate behavior. She was even more surprised when I introduced her to the boy and explained that Fania had just arrived from the Soviet Union and was my bride. The boy was thrilled; he ran to his friends, told them the news, and soon a group of boys started loudly singing a song about a bride and groom in Hebrew. I hurriedly took Fania inside to the staff room. My colleagues' reception of Fania was warm, and they congratulated her on coming to Israel. I was a happy translator, helping teachers and Fania communicate with each other.

Fania and I went to the Jerusalem branch of the Jewish Agency to ask for their help in placing her in some ulpan or other school to learn Hebrew, but our effort was futile. It was too close to the end of the school year, and all ulpans would be closed for summer; we had no choice but to wait. After my workdays, we would go to the city center to see the shops and the streets of Jerusalem lit up at night. On weekends, we ventured into the Old City, with its Middle Eastern markets and scent of spices and shish-kebabs. A few times, we visited the Western Wall, where hundreds of Jews were praying. We also walked into the Christian church where Jesus had been buried.

These places were both exotic and peaceful for us: Jews and Arabs were busy praying and doing their business without venturing into politics. Later, I had an improbable encounter at the Wall: I bumped into Vladimir M., the random stranger to whom I had lent money in Moscow and who kept his promise to pay me back. How strange to see him in Jerusalem.

One day, I took Fania to Mount Scopus to show her where I was teaching my university students. From there, she enjoyed a breathtaking view of the Old City and the golden top of the Dome of the Rock standing where the Jewish Second Temple had stood 2,000 years ago. At that time, Jerusalem was composed of separate neighborhoods that seemed to be sprinkled on the hills and connected by roads. Jerusalem's buildings were clad with yellowish Jerusalem stones to blend into the land's desert-like emptiness with ease. We could feel the spirit of more than 3,500 years of history of this special land. The biblical past and its connection to the unknown future were in the air, which filled our hearts with trepidation and awe. I have never had this kind of feeling in any other place.

Every day, Fania learned something new about life in Israel and Jerusalem. We cooked together, spent time together, and observed each other. I felt that the question of where we were going in terms of our relationship from here would come up, but I wasn't sure what I wanted. I was confused. I was keenly aware of my responsibility for Fania, but I also wanted to know her better as a human being before making a commitment. I saw that, after a month of living in my room and sleeping on my bed while I slept on the floor, Fania had become very sad. I tried a few times to have a conversation with her about my feelings, but it only made the situation worse. Fania was occupying more of my heart every day—but I was scared.

Finally, toward the end of May, it was time to overcome my fear and make the right decision. I asked Fania to marry me, and she happily agreed. It had taken us more than a year and a half from the moment in Moscow when we'd met to the moment we decided to build our home and future together. It was a huge relief for me; my inner turmoil was gone. I let my love for Fania spill over and showed her my affection.

We decided to marry as soon as possible because I wanted to be recruited to the short three-month army training (instead of the longer army service required of younger unmarried men) during the summer so that I could return to my teaching job at university at the beginning of the next school year. Our reason for marrying when we did wasn't particularly romantic—but there was love involved.

I went to the Office of the Chief Rabbinate to register for the wedding and get information on any formalities associated with our marriage. There we ran into a funny but sad situation: in Israel, all Jewish marriages were conducted under the jurisdiction of the Orthodox branch of Judaism, and they had stringent rules. First, both of us had to prove that we were Jewish. That was no problem for me: my Israeli cousins and Aunt Zipora were able to confirm this fact by phone; also, they had found my record of circumcision. The problem was with Fania. She had no family in Israel and didn't know anyone from Frunze who could confirm her pedigree. We started asking our friends and, after two weeks, she found two people who were ready to sign a document confirming that Fania was, in fact, Jewish. We received our wedding date—July 5, 1973.

Because it was only two days before final exams, I had to work until two o'clock on the day of the wedding. Then I went to Hannah and Michael Ratner's apartment to meet Fania and my friends, who were already in the midst of preparing for the big event. After borrowing Michael's suit (I didn't have one), tie, and socks, I was ready to go, and we had no time to waste before driving to the Chief Rabbinate Office in Jerusalem's downtown. Many guests were already present. The pre-wedding ceremony included filling in a *ketuba* (marriage contract) as per ancient tradition, then having it signed by witnesses. At 5:30 p.m., we had a short ceremony under a *chuppah* (canopy). After the rabbis had finished their prayers and read the contents of the ketuba to the participating public, and after Fania and I exchanged rings, I stamped on a glass cup (in memory of the Jewish temple that the Romans destroyed) and the ceremony was over.

A long table by the wall of the auditorium was laden with sandwiches, soft drinks, cookies and cakes, and challah bread. Somebody put on traditional wedding music and everyone began dancing: a few of my comrades from the Odesa dissident group, teachers from my school, my university students, friends from Shtern Street, and my Israeli relatives; even shy Ilya Rips took to the floor. It was a simple wedding party, and we had to finish by 7 p.m. as another wedding ceremony was scheduled after us.

Clearly, Fania missed her family. There was no doubt in my mind that the finality of leaving behind her mother (whom she never saw again) and brothers was difficult for her. After we married, I learned a lot about Fania's struggles growing up. Her parents were born and raised in a small town near the Ukrainian city of Vinnitsa. Her father, Isaak Shtramvasser, was a textile machinery engineer in a large factory. When the Germans invaded the Soviet Union in 1941, the textile factory and management staff were evacuated east to the Soviet Republic of Kyrgyzstan. This move saved the Shtramvassers and their young son from the horrors of the Holocaust. The family stayed in Frunze, the capital of Kyrgyzstan, after World War II. Fania and her second brother were born there.

After Fania's father had been made head of the shop in Frunze, he and a colleague came up with a way of producing items that were badly needed, but unavailable in Soviet markets, using textile remnants that were usually thrown away and obsolete machinery, which they refurbished. In any normal country, this kind of initiative would have been welcomed; however, in the Soviet Union any economic initiative operating outside the framework established by the Communist Party—however reasonable and beneficial it was for the people—was illegal. Of course, this niche production had been established in collaboration with city officials, the local government of Kyrgyzstan, and officials in product distribution centers, who happily partook of the black market profits.

It wasn't without risk, however. Eventually, someone who stood to benefit from exposing the operation reported it to the KGB, which always welcomed the chance to demonstrate its power. In January 1961 hundreds of people were arrested in Kyrgyzstan and Russia for being involved in these kinds of side hustles, of which there were many. In the government newspaper *Sovetskaya Kirghizia* on January 9, 1962, Fania's father was identified as a member of a "gang of embezzlers." Most of the people arrested were given death sentences. Many of those executed—including Fania's father—were Jews. Afterwards, his body, along with those of others executed by Khrushchev, disappeared; the bodies were never given to their families and, to date, nobody knows where the graves are.[3] Fania and her family suffered from this loss, but the KGB's punishment didn't end there; they were relegated to complete poverty and living conditions that were anything but livable.

---

3   To give a more complete picture of Soviet criminal law, here are some facts: (a) in 1962 alone, more than three thousand people received the death sentence in the USSR (Soviet law was used retroactively when it was convenient for the communists); (b) fourteen new laws were created to allow death sentences for such crimes as economic disobedience, political deviation, and attempting to run away from the Soviet paradise; and (c) about 24,000 people were sentenced to death in the USSR between 1962 and 1990.

Reuven's father-in-law Isaak Shtramvasser, executed for economic crimes in 1962. Article in the Russian-language American newspaper *Novoye Russkoye Slovo*, April 26, 1996.

The Israeli Army

I had to leave her just ten days after our wedding: I took a bus from Jerusalem to Netanya, where my new military unit was to assemble the next morning. In a prior interview with the army draft office, I learned that because I was an immigrant, had been in the Red Army, held a university degree, and was past the age of twenty-five, I would be required to serve at *shlav Bet* (stage two) for only three months. When asked about the kind of military unit I wanted to join, I shared my desire to work as an air force radio and radar tech or, alternatively, in a communications unit. The officer who processed me started laughing and told me to forget the air force because I was a newcomer from the Soviet Union, which was decidedly not friendly with Israel. Because of my mathematical background, he said that I would join the artillery unit after training. I shared my rather sad (but understandable) story with the officer: I hadn't been allowed to attend pilot school in the Red Army because I was a Jew; now I couldn't serve in the Israeli air force because I was "Russian."

When I arrived in Netanya, in July 1973, I was told to assemble on the outskirts of town, near the walls of a large prison. From there, buses took us to a base near Shechem (the Palestinian city of Nablus). The military base was on top of a hill overlooking the town below. The headquarters building was in the middle of the base; soldiers were housed in tents (each comprised of ten men) around it. After changing into uniforms, we began our initial general training (*tironut*), which emphasized physical strength and taught us how to handle and shoot weapons, along with the army's rules and regulations. I had a great surprise: Izia Rashkovsky, my comrade from Odesa, was assigned to my tent, as were a few other Russian-speaking guys and a few Moroccans from south Tel Aviv. During the month and a half of being stationed in Shechem, I was granted two two-day visits with Fania; they were the sweetest in my life.

I spent the last month and a half learning artillery near Tel Aviv. After a few weeks of training, a new group of young soldiers arrived for officer training. These young men were around eighteen, had just graduated from high school, and had already completed their three months in tironut. Among the group was Rami, the oldest son of my cousin Reuven. We had a little chat, and I would see him whenever we were free.

It took more than a month to learn our new military profession. I was allowed to go home for a few days several times. Many guys from our group had to go home from October 5 to 7, Friday to Sunday, to observe Yom Kippur. Our graduation was scheduled for the morning of October 8. After that, we were to return to our civilian lives. However, when we tried to depart, we were ordered back to barracks.

We had nothing to do that evening other than speculate on why we were being kept back. As it started getting dark, the trainee officers who'd arrived with Rami were loaded onto buses—but Rami wasn't permitted to tell me where they were going. We were awakened early the next morning by a loud siren. We all crashed out of our tents, realizing that something was terribly wrong. As the officers were running to headquarters, one of them stopped and announced that the Egyptians and Syrians had executed a surprise attack on Israel and war had begun: we were officially in an emergency situation. The officer responsible for our group told me that the cadets who'd left the evening before, including Rami, were now in Sinai.

Soon our base was flooded with reservists: some were taken by buses to places where they would receive arms and cannons; others stayed with us to learn how to use the Soviet cannons that had been captured during the Six Day War and how to fire Soviet guns. Russian-speaking new artillery specialists were given instruction manuals in Russian to translate and explain to Israeli reservists. We asked why we had to use this archaic Soviet weaponry. The answer was that Israel wasn't ready for the war and didn't have enough equipment to fight the attacking armies. It took two or three days for the reservists to learn the differences between American and Soviet cannons.

In the midst of all this I was ordered to the front gate, where I found Fania with an army major. We spent a few wonderful hours together, and then she took a taxi back to Jerusalem. The next day, another officer gave me some horrible news: Egyptian warplanes had bombed Rami's group upon their arrival in Sinai; severely injured in the chest and arm, Rami had been airlifted to a hospital near Tel Aviv.

My unit was ready to go to the front lines, and I had to go too. But as we started driving on the highway, our commander received an order for us to return to our base. The Syrian army had progressed quickly on the Golan Heights and captured the warehouse that held the shells for our cannons. I spent another few days worrying about Fania being alone in Jerusalem and about the problems on the front lines in the south and the north of Israel. We had a TV in the base's club room; we were glued to it every free minute we had.

Before I was assigned to a new unit, one of the guys from the tank unit, my neighbor from Shtern Street, got back to the base from the Golan Heights. He was walking strangely, as though after a major shock, his eyes wide open. I asked him what was going on. He told me that nearly his whole unit was dead. They'd gone to a position to fight advancing Syrian tanks. Arriving in the dark, they saw tanks already there. The officer in charge assumed that they were Israeli tanks. He called out in Hebrew to ask what tank unit it was. Unfortunately, however, they were Syrian tanks, which fired on them from close range. All the Israeli tanks—along with a few commanders' cars—were hit. My neighbor had survived, but only after having been thrown from his tank, hiding in a ditch, and rolling into a ravine. Finally, at night, they reached another Israeli position. From there, my friend had been sent back to our base.

After the first few days of the war, Israel was running out of heavy equipment and ammunition. It was evident that the country wasn't properly prepared for war. People were stressed and started losing confidence in the government. The United States delayed supplying us with badly needed equipment, and we were losing lots of lives because of it. Finally, we saw numerous large American transport planes landing at Lod Airport to deliver supplies. Every fifteen minutes, another plane would fly above our base and touch down. This improved our morale greatly. Everyone wanted to fight to defend our country, but it wasn't easy without modern technology and sufficient ammunition.

I was ordered to join another unit of reservists going south to the Sinai. We were bused to the artillery warehouse in the Negev Desert and lifted the necessary heavy mortars onto the French tank platform. After a day of trials in the desert, we rolled our tanks onto tractor trailers to move out to the Sinai. Our mortars could reach two or three miles, so we supported other fighting units from the rear. My job was to line up our four tanks, calculate angles and the amount of explosive for our shells, and make corrections if the target wasn't hit. After hitting the enemy target with our first shell, we had ten or fifteen minutes for our other cannons to shoot the same place. Then we changed our position to avoid being hit by return fire. There was no time to think about myself; there was too much adrenaline. We slept at night beside our tanks.

In October, nights in the Sinai Desert were quite cold, and I wasn't dressed warmly enough. I awoke one morning with a high fever: I couldn't run and my hands trembled. I asked our medic to give me some medicine, but after listening to my lungs, he said that I probably had pneumonia; so, he ordered me to go to our division's medical center (about a third of a mile from our position), and he called to ensure that a medical duty officer was expecting me. By the time I arrived, I was utterly exhausted. The medical officer checked me more thoroughly; my temperature was nearly 102°F. He ordered me to rest, and I would be airlifted to a hospital in Be'er Sheva. From there, I was sent (on my own) to Jerusalem by bus: the hospital was filled with wounded soldiers, so no one had time for my supposedly trivial problem.

When I arrived at the city's central bus station about three hours later, I fell on the ground (holding my army backpack and rifle) and almost lost consciousness. People ran to help me. Fortunately, one of them was my neighbor in the building on Shtern Street, who recognized me and helped me to get home. He called Fania, and she took care of me. At night, my temperature rose to almost 104 degrees, so, as per the instructions from the Be'er Sheva hospital, Fania called a military ambulance. The medic inspected me, gave me some medication, and took me to Hadassah Hospital, which wasn't far from where we lived. I had a bed in a shared room with some sick civilians. Wounded soldiers were hospitalized in another wing dealing with shrapnel wounds, burns, and other severe injuries. Fania and I spent a few hours together, and then she took a taxi home. I sat out the rest of the war, which ended on October 25, in the hospital.

Return to Civilian Life

I had plenty of time to work on my doctoral thesis and read books while in the hospital. At the same time, many things were happening at home. Fania applied for, and received, an apartment sponsored by the Jewish Agency. My parents and my brother Izia arrived in Israel on January 1, 1974; but because nobody had let us know about their arrival, they were forced to take a taxi to my Aunt Zipora's home in Petah Tikva. They stayed for a week until they moved to Fania's in Jerusalem. She'd made the apartment spotless and comfortable. I had another two weeks in hospital still, until my lungs were clear of the pneumonia. I had been placed on reserve duty with the army, and so I was eventually able to see my family.

Convalescing in the hospital had some perks—and while likely not a welcomed pastime for most others, I was able to think about math! One day, suddenly, out of the blue, I knew how to prove the last—but central—theorem of my thesis. Everything fell into place. All I had left to do was create a few examples supporting my theory. I finished them in a few weeks and was ready to publish the summary of my work. I needed to translate my thesis into English (I had written it in Russian) and get approval from Professor Agmon before sending it to the printer. I contacted Liza, a math teacher at the school, and asked her if she could help me. She was perfect because she spoke good English and Russian and had a bachelor's degree in math. We started working on this final step in September, at the start of the school year; and we completed it in just two weeks. Professor Agmon read my work for about an hour and gave me the green light. After that, I delivered my thesis to the university's print shop. Mission accomplished. My long-awaited dream had come to pass: I had finally earned my PhD in math!

I returned to my work at the school and settled into the routine. Then, in April 1975, I received another summons to reserve duty for three weeks in May. I'd been working hard, but it wasn't particularly arduous. Dr. Kirshenbaum nudged me to plan something special to showcase the math enrichment program and its students—something that would entertain students and parents alike, something unusual. After some soul-searching and some thought, I decided to organize a special "Logician-Mathematician" event. After speaking and negotiating with all my students, we outlined the scope and nature of the special event and started working on its parts: game booths and funny and entertaining math problems for all attending. After two months of preparation, we were ready to invite other students and parents for the grand event. One of my classes wrote and performed *Mama Algebra and Papa Geometry*—a fantastic, and funny, theatrical production. The parents loved our students' ingenuity and passion, happiness and joy, as well as their excitement for all things mathematical, of course. I was surprised by how much the kids could accomplish when they put effort into something they loved!

At home, however, things were taking a turn for the worse; Fania told me that she'd tripped and fell on her back when rushing to work one winter day. While this would have been awful on its own, it was doubly so because she was pregnant. As a result of the accident, she'd had some bleeding and was taken to hospital. The doctors tried to save our baby by performing a surgery to prevent a premature delivery. She was in and out of the hospital for a time, and I was with her as much as my work schedule allowed. One night, I received a call from the hospital informing me that Fania was in the delivery room after another bleeding event. After only seven months, our baby had decided to come out early; by morning, Fania had delivered a premature boy. When I arrived at the hospital, our tiny son was in an incubator and Fania was devastated and weeping in bed.

I looked at our son through the window and saw a little Shtramvasser. He was Fania's—he had very similar facial features. Moving his hands and legs, he was so small and defenseless, attached to so many tubes. I started crying. The doctors kept Fania under observation for a few days. Three or four days after the delivery, I went to the hospital in the morning to be with her. Our son wasn't in the room where all the newborn babies were kept. Fania was in bed crying and unable to speak. I asked the nurse what was going on, and she told me that our son had died during the night. I sat beside Fania, held her hands, hugged her, and felt a sharp pain in my heart. When I came home, I pulled out a bottle of vodka, poured myself a glass, and drank it to dull my pain. Our neighbor Ida (she'd provided Fania with her wedding dress) and her husband came to the apartment to look after me and calm me down. I was heartbroken. For many years after, I was haunted by the image of that tiny baby boy lying in an incubator, attached to machines by tubes and wires, moving his hands and legs as though he were begging for help. This event devastated us for many years, and we were very unhappy in Israel.

I brought Fania home a few days later; both of us had to deal with the trauma. It was a tough time for both of us. I don't remember getting much support from my family. Izia was studying at Tel Aviv University. Hanna was an elementary and junior high biology and arts teacher near Netanya. My parents had just settled into their jobs in Petah Tikva; they had no time and no car to travel to Jerusalem to visit us. We were very isolated.

Of course, a twist of fate and an exit from the trauma was just around the corner. Early one morning, as I was heading in to teach, a man stopped me at my classroom door, presented himself as a professor at the Hebrew University and as the father of one of my best students. He then asked a strange question: Would I like to teach at an Israeli school in Paris for a few years? I was completely surprised and didn't know what to say—it must be a joke, I thought. I told him that I had to talk to my wife and we shook hands. I entered the classroom and soon forgot about the encounter.

When I went home that evening after a long day of preparing students from our high school division for their graduation exams in calculus, I remembered the professor and told Fania about his proposal. She was eager to know what I'd said. I told her that I'd been so astonished that I hadn't asked anything, such as: Why me? What are the details? I told Fania that it didn't seem real and that I hadn't taken it seriously. When she pressed me, I remembered telling him that I needed to talk to my wife.

Fania looked at me with disdain. I'll never forget her words (albeit, they were said gently): "Reuven, you must be a stupid man for not saying yes immediately. We might have missed a wonderful opportunity to see the world." She called me a *schlimazel* (an endearing loser). Then she asked me if I had the professor's phone number to call him and agree to take up the post. I didn't have his name, address, or phone number. I still didn't believe that the offer was for real: after all, I was a newcomer to the country, my Hebrew was still broken, and I spoke with a strong Russian accent. A job teaching at an Israeli school abroad was surely open to the Israeli elite only. The whole idea was ridiculous.

A week later, I joined my unit in Sinai and forgot about everything. It was scorching in the sandy western part of the peninsular during the daytime, so we didn't do much when the sun was out. Our training exercises were mainly in the evenings and at night. There wasn't much stress, the desert was peaceful, and reserve duty was like being at a sports camp. In the middle of the second week, a phone line was set up so that we could call home. Fania told me that she had been visited by two odd gentlemen a few days earlier. They'd asked about my whereabouts and notified me that a meeting was scheduled at the Hebrew University at the end of May with the principal of the school in Paris. She begged me not to be a schlimazel again and to think seriously about this excellent opportunity.

When I was finally released from the reserves, I went back to teaching. After a few days, Adi, one of my best students, gave me a piece of paper with a telephone number on it and told me that his father wanted me to call him in the evening. Adi's father was Professor Haim Rosen from the Linguistics

Department at the Hebrew University. After a few pleasantries, he told me that he was aware of my scheduled meeting with the school principal and suggested that we meet beforehand so that he could prepare me and tell me more about his plans for the coming year. Fania overheard this conversation and suggested that we invite Haim Rosen and his wife to our place later that week.

As we shared food and wine, Haim explained that he was taking a sabbatical the following year and was heading to Paris. There would be a few significant events in the city, and he wanted to do some research there as well. However, Adi categorically didn't want to go with him; he liked the after-school math program that I had set up. To overcome his son's resistance, Haim had contacted the Israeli school, spoken with the principal to inform him of the work I was doing with students in Jerusalem, and proposed that this program could be run in Paris if I was there. Since he was looking for a math teacher for the next school year, the principal was very interested. And he was coming to Jerusalem to meet me; if I impressed him, he would offer me the job. Haim gave me some valuable advice about what to say and how to present myself. We had an enjoyable time at our place. Haim and Hannah were amiable; we began a warm friendship with the Rosen family that evening.

On the appointed date, I met with the principal and a man who worked at the Israeli embassy in Paris (he didn't explain why he was at the meeting). The principal was a nice, intelligent guy with a PhD in literature. He was originally from a North African country and slightly older than me. We had a lovely two-hour-long chat. Both men were interested in my education, life in the Soviet Union, military service there, my move to Israel, my work in Jerusalem, and, of course, my fighting in the Yom Kippur War. At the end of our meeting, the principal told me about the working conditions at the school and promised to send me a job offer in a few days.

Haim called me the same evening and I reported my impressions to him. He told me that he would expedite the school's decision—and he really did. I received an official job offer a few days later. Again, I turned to Haim, who advised me to: (a) ask for a sabbatical from my current teaching job; (b) obtain a release from reserve duties; (c) get release letters from the bank and the Jewish Agency; and (d) get the required passports, travel documents, and various papers. Since neither Fania nor I had traveled outside of the Soviet Union and Israel, he suggested that we travel with him and his family to Paris in mid-July. Haim and Hannah were very familiar with Europe. He assured me that we had enough time to prepare for the trip, and we agreed to call each other periodically to check that everything was moving along smoothly.

The first item on my to-do list was to tell Dr. Kirshenbaum about my leaving and ask him to authorize my "sabbatical." He was taken by surprise when I showed him my job offer. He asked me why a newcomer was being offered such a job when there were hundreds of Israeli-born teachers with perfect Hebrew. They would kill to work in Paris. What had I done to be invited to such a prestigious school? I told him that it was word of mouth. The Paris school had heard about my extracurricular program and they wanted me to run it there. As Dr. Kirshenbaum couldn't grant me a two- or three-year-long sabbatical, I was pretty much free to go to Paris for a while. Then I met with the vice principal, Michal Orev. She became sad when I told her and speculated that I probably wouldn't come back after completing my stint in France. From her experience, not many people returned to Israel after getting a taste of life in Europe or America.

My next stop was the Jewish Agency office. I was still a newcomer; it had made it easier for me to buy a car, apartment, appliances, and other items. I needed a letter specifying that I didn't owe anything to the agency or the Israeli government. I filled out the required forms and a clerk asked me to come back in a few days to obtain either our release papers or information about our debts. When I went back, I found that I needed to repay the money I'd received from the Dutch embassy in Moscow (with which I'd paid off the Soviet government for my education and for renouncing my citizenship); the cost of the ulpan in Jerusalem; and other smaller sums for household items I had bought with a newcomer's reduced tax rate. In all, Fania and I had to repay a sizable amount and needed to determine how we would find the funds to do so.

To get a release from my reserve duties, I called my unit's commander. It was easy: because of the timing of my next round of duty, they were able to release me in June. At the beginning of July, we planned to go to the government offices to apply for passports and travel documents, to the central post office, and to the teachers' bank. On the way to the post office, we heard a thunderous boom and people's screams as we turned right on Zion Square. There'd been an explosion behind us: body parts were flying all around us; we were covered in other people's blood; people were running away from the square; and bodies were scattered everywhere. Fania was paralyzed with extreme shock. She could neither move nor talk: tears were running down her frightened face. She was in a terrible state. I put her over my shoulder and ran with her back to our lawyer's office on Ben Yehuda Street, where she lay trembling on a sofa. I gave her water to drink, and after an hour we went back to our car. She was still recovering from the shock of losing our firstborn; the explosion left her barely functioning.

Later we learned that it was a terrorist attack. The perpetrators had packed a refrigerator with explosives, nails, and bolts to maximize damage. More than a dozen people were killed that morning and more than sixty were injured. Palestinian terror groups were targeting Jerusalem. They put numerous bombs in the city's garbage cans, loaded bicycles with explosives and left them on the streets, and hid explosives in shopping bags at bus stops. The terrorists targeted innocents—women and children in particular. There were a few mornings when we found suspicious bags on the floor outside our apartment and called the police. It was stressful in Jerusalem, but we coped. The explosion that day, though, was too much for Fania: it took her several days to return to normal, although I'm not sure that she ever really recovered fully. I don't think I did. I'm not sure anyone does.

We had a few days left before departure. We went to Petah Tikva, where my parents were then living, to say goodbye. We sat with my parents at their apartment, explained to them that I was going to Paris to work at the school at the Israeli embassy, and that we would be back in two or three years. My mother sat quietly and didn't ask many questions about our plans in Europe; my father, though, became very upset. In his mind, anyone sent to work abroad by the government had to be a spy, so he assumed that I wasn't being truthful, that I was a spy. Fania and I chose not to argue and left him to think whatever he wanted.

France

On the morning of departure, Haim, Hannah, and Adi Rosen came to our building in their Peugeot. We waited for them in our Audi 80, and our little caravan drove to Haifa's port. We passed all the checks and drove onto the ship to Europe.

The school year started at the beginning of September; I taught classes with well-behaved students. Fania stayed at home while I was at work. After school, I had to grade assignments, prepare the next day's classes, and help her. To compensate for her being home alone during weekdays, we spent many weekends exploring Paris.

I was teaching math in Hebrew, as it was an Israeli school. Relationships with my colleagues were good, but Fania and I developed a special relationship with the school's principal, Palti, and his family. The only thing that really bothered us in those days was our very poor, rudimentary French. So we signed up for French language classes at the Alliance Française. Twice a week, we took the subway there in the evenings and sat in a class of about twenty students. I liked these evenings—except for trying to write the small pieces which were dictated by the professor. However, we started understanding and handling conversations in French, following French-language television, and reading newspapers and simple books.

My first year of teaching passed quickly. That summer was busy. We often had visitors from Israel because Paris was one of the main attractions for Israelis traveling abroad. One day we received a phone call from Michael and Rima Barenboim from Petah Tikva, who had helped me so much when I arrived in Israel and who'd become close friends after our wedding. They were flying to New York and hoped to stay with me and Fania in Paris for a few days so that we could catch up and show them the city. We were happy to accommodate them. At the appointed time, we picked them up from the airport, brought them to our tiny studio apartment, and spent a few beautiful days walking around different parts of Paris. They had officially left Israel and were emigrating to the United States. On their last day, Rima gave her pearl earrings to Fania and hugged her. They cried a bit, but then Michael and Rima insisted that we visit them in New York after they were settled there.

We received an invitation to my brother Haim's wedding in Israel in June 1976. I couldn't go, though, because it was during preparation for the yearly exams, among other obligations; but we decided that Fania would attend. She left for Israel and was scheduled to return to Paris on June 27. In a crazy twist of fate, while I was getting ready to head to the airport to greet her, I received a message from the embassy that terrorists had hijacked an Air France plane and taken it to Entebbe, in Uganda. I was so scared, as I was sure that she had taken this flight. A friend of mine came to be with me that evening; I was in quite a state. I tried to go to the embassy to get the latest news, but the French police blocked all of the streets leading to it. I could see from a distance that people were going in and out of the embassy, some commotion was happening, but I couldn't get close. My friend offered to take me on a drive, but afterwards, I still couldn't get any information about Fania. I went back to our apartment in the early morning, but couldn't sleep: I was certain Fania was in trouble.

Later in the morning, I received a phone call from her telling me she'd missed the plane and was coming to Paris on the next El Al flight. The phone lines were jammed, so she hadn't been able to reach me sooner. I was so relieved! We'd barely escaped a catastrophic situation—she had a ticket for the hijacked flight in her hand. Even after Fania was safely home, we were glued to our television watching events unfold. About a week later, the Israeli Special Service Unit freed most of the hostages, losing one soldier and only a few passengers.[4] This would become known as the famous "Operation Thunderbolt" mission—often touted as a brilliantly planned and perfectly executed hostage rescue and perhaps the most daring such rescue mission in history.

There were more than two weeks until the start of the new school year. I started working on my yearly lesson plans and other preparations as a classroom teacher. One evening we got a call from Palti; he invited us to go out with him and his wife. As we were strolling on the Champs-Élysées, with the two women walking ahead of us, Palti asked me if I would take the position of vice principal at the school. His offer took me by surprise: I had no such ambitions and I knew that a few more mature Israeli teachers were desperate for the job and would be offended at not being offered it. Palti told me that there was lots of political infighting among the teachers and that he didn't trust them. Moreover, he had observed me during my first year at the school and decided that I could be trusted and would do well in the job. I sensed that it would be a tumultuous year for me, but I used the opportunity to ask if there was an opening in our kindergarten so that Fania could also work at the school. Palti answered that he was looking for a kindergarten teacher and two assistants. He asked Fania to fill out an application, and he would take care of it.

My new responsibility was to oversee the math programs in all of the grades, plan yearly schedules for all subjects, classes, and teachers, transport students to and from school, supervise the work done by the school superintendent, and assist the security personnel. In my new position, I quickly learned how the school operated under the strict supervision of the embassy. Because of my new position, I could also buy duty-free items (such as cigarettes and liquor) from the embassy shop.

---

4   There have been multiple critically acclaimed movies and books made on this historical event; for example, most recently the 2018 film 7 Days in Entebbe: https://www.youtube.com/watch?v=kuTBea8_-LY. Please also see: https://en.wikipedia.org/wiki/Entebbe_raid

At the start of the school year, Fania and I worked in the same building. We had several opportunities to see each other during the day and even ate our lunch together. She loved working with little ones and enjoyed a good relationship with the kindergarten staff. On weekends and holidays, we would explore Paris or drive to the forest area outside of the city. During this time, I read a variety of books by Soviet dissidents that had been prohibited in the USSR but were published in the West.

We kept up with Michael and Rima, and they reminded us about our promise to visit them in New York. A few weeks before Passover, Fania found an ad in a newspaper about special Passover fares to New York. We had two weeks off for the holiday, so we jumped at the opportunity to see our friends and America. We took off on the last day before the holiday and Michael met us in New York. He took us to Queens, where they lived in a rental apartment with their kids and Rima's parents. We had a lovely time with them all. Michael and Rima took us to different parts of the city: we visited the Statue of Liberty, Brooklyn, Central Park, and other notable places. Everything was exciting. Nonetheless, we became depressed at the sight of many abandoned buildings, dirty streets, and beggars. The city—seemingly so impoverished— was the antithesis of Paris.

A few days after our arrival in New York, we received a phone call from Toronto. The callers said they were relatives of a woman in Kyrgyzstan who was good friends with Fania's mother. They invited us to visit them for a few days. They told us they had spoken with Fania's mom when they'd called their relative in Frunze. We accepted their invitation and took a train to Toronto the next day. A couple met us at Toronto's railway station and took us to their home. Abrasha Mendlowitz was a Polish Jew who had fled from the Nazis to the Soviet Union in 1940. He spent a few years in Siberia cutting down trees and sewing uniforms for the military, and met and married Zina, a Russian Jewish girl. In 1946, they'd began a series of moves (including a stay in Cyprus as refugees and a period in the newly formed State of Israel that sadly coincided with the Arab-Israeli War). The war ultimately led them to join Abrasha's brother in Canada.

Once in Canada, Abrasha and Zina had worked in a factory for a few years and then bought a small convenience store which took up all of their time but afforded them a comfortable living. Their son was a high school student, and their daughter was married to a man who—when we visited in 1977—was studying law at the University of Toronto (U of T). While we were there, we shared lovely Passover dinners with Abrasha and Zina's family and friends. Their daughter and her husband took us to the U of T campus, the Ontario Parliament building, downtown, and other places. We were impressed by the city's cleanliness, the politeness of the people, and the number of beautiful parks and children's playgrounds. The air in Toronto was fresh, cool, and crisp—a marked contrast with New York.

One day, Zina and Abrasha told us that we were invited for lunch at the home of Rabbi Lipsker from the Chabad Lubavich organization. Rabbi Lipsker asked us many questions about who we were, our parents, our education, and how we got out of the USSR. The rabbi—who had managed to leave the USSR just after World War II—was very active in Chabad in Toronto, was a teacher in the Chabad school, and spoke Russian.

At the end of lunch, Rabbi Lipsker told us that he knew about us from Chabad in Paris and asked me if I would be willing to come to Toronto to work with Chabad to help new Russian Jews enter the Jewish community. He said that Canada was expecting a lot of new Russian Jewish immigrants who, because of restrictions on religious studies in the USSR, would be mostly secular and unfamiliar with Judaism. Chabad was looking for a Russian-speaker who knew the religion and traditions and could organize a school for kids. He felt that I would be a good candidate for the job and, if I was interested, he would discuss it with his superiors. Again, I had to ask Fania if this was appealing; she told me that we could always return to Israel, but that we wouldn't get another offer like this. So we gave Rabbi Lipsker our consent to proceed.

When we returned to New York, Michael and Rima suggested we come live in the United States; they were willing to help us and provide the personal grant required to support our immigration. We told them about our invitation to Canada and our impressions of Toronto. We explained why I'd accepted the job and reassured them that, with only a one-hour flight between Toronto and New York, we'd be able to visit each other often. Though they were disappointed, Michael offered me some solid advice: he gave me a thick book about programming in Cobol and suggested that learning it might be helpful in the future.

Back in Paris, we continued our work routine. We soon received a letter from Chabad in Toronto notifying us that they had started the formal process of inviting me to work for them. It was a long process—they first had to establish that there were no other appropriate candidates living in the country, but they anticipated approval by late spring or early summer. They hoped to greet us in August 1978.

We talked with Michael and Rima frequently and told them that we were expecting papers for emigration to Canada. They were still disappointed, and once again advised me to take a programming course, just in case there were any troubles at Chabad. After a few phone calls with them, I signed up for a two-month evening course. Michael's suggestion proved to be quite useful once I was living in Canada.

That school year was full of surprises—some better than others. It was the year my father passed away. On December 4, 1977, I received a phone call from my family about his tragic death in Israel. The funeral was scheduled for the following day, but I could not leave Fania alone. Even if she could have been left alone for a week, it was too late for me to fly to Israel for the funeral. So, instead, I went to synagogue and ordered the reading of Kaddish for thirty days, as per Jewish tradition. My father was killed by a bus one early morning when he was going to work. It had been very foggy, so nobody saw how it happened; it was a hit and run.

Yet 1977 was also the year I learned Fania was pregnant again—I would finally become a father. This time we were hopeful that we would be able to start our little family. We had a phenomenal doctor, Dr. Ravina of Hôpital Bichat. At one point, although he was not Jewish and likely did not know about kashrut, he recommended that Fania avoid eating pork and shellfish, as it was healthier for the fetus. We were taken aback. These foods weren't kosher either, yet we'd never thought of abandoning them until the doctor had mentioned them! Dr. Ravina's suggestion caused us to pause and reflect; ultimately, we decided to permanently give up a lot of nonkosher foods. It was a turning point for us in terms of our interest in tradition and religion.

The baby was due in May, and my mom was coming to visit us to be there for the delivery. She also was joining us to find comfort and solace, as she was still mourning my father. Despite some hiccups (she arrived late and got lost!) and the baby's (late and reluctant!) entrance into the world, our little girl was born. She was healthy and red-headed, and barely cried. It was an exciting moment, and I could not wait to take our baby home to our place in La Defense. When obtaining her French birth certificate and selecting a name for her, I made certain to choose something that wouldn't put her in the predicament I'd endured as a child. Her name would be something beautiful, French, and not obviously Jewish. We chose the name Karine.

The Tel Aviv Board of Education supervised the Paris school. That year I was responsible for working with one of its inspectors for about two weeks. She reviewed our staff profiles and administrative paperwork and observed every teacher's lessons. While I was working very hard to prove that we provided a high-quality education, Fania was at home caring for Karine. The inspector also asked me to show her the city in the evenings, which I had been assigned to do by the principal.

At the end of her visit, the inspector and I met one last time. She thanked me for all the time and effort I'd dedicated to her. She knew that we had a newborn baby and said she was touched that I had given her so much of my free time. She opened a map of Tel Aviv on which various areas of the city were highlighted and said that I could work in any one of the schools marked on the map. Most of these positions were at the vice principal level, but a few schools needed principals. She told me to think about it and let her know by the end of July. My contract in Paris would expire at the end of June. Theoretically, Fania and I had to return home to Israel in July or the beginning of August. I promised to call her.

Later in June, we got another letter from Chabad Toronto notifying us that they were still proving that I was uniquely qualified for the job; as soon as the Canadian government approved my application, I would be notified to make an appointment at Canada's embassy in Paris. However, we still hadn't had any further news from Canada by the end of June, so I started to worry about our situation. We had to leave France in a few months. Potentially, there was an excellent job waiting for me in Tel Aviv, but we were waiting for our papers for Canada, and we had no idea how long it would take. So Fania and I decided to ask our school to allow her to work there for a few months in the new school year until I had completed the postdoctoral research I was doing at the Sorbonne. We spent the summer of 1978 in Paris taking care of Karine, then, spending time with friends and communicating with our friends in Canada. During a phone call, Abrasha and Zina told us that our process had stalled because Chabad had run into some problem proving my uniqueness for the job. However, they felt that it was temporary and that we'd get the green light in a month or two.

In September, Fania went back to work at the school's kindergarten while I stayed home with Karine. I drew from all my experience looking after my siblings when they were babies. After lunch, I usually wheeled her to the Esplanade in La Défense, about a ten-minute walk from our building, where we would stroll around looking at the fountains, the construction site of a future entertainment center, and new buildings. I would sit on one of the benches reading a magazine or book for a while and then take another walk before Fania came home from work. For some reason (because of my sense of traditional gender roles?) I didn't feel comfortable when she was at work and I was stuck at home; however, we knew that this arrangement was needed for a couple of months.

Reuven with his daughter Karine in Paris.

Fania and I decided that if we didn't get our papers from Canada before the new year, we would return to Israel. But in mid-September, another letter from Chabad Toronto arrived; it said that all the obstacles to immigration had been cleared. It was time to make an appointment with the Canadian embassy in Paris. We filled out a set of forms and were interviewed—half in English, the rest in French. Fortunately, we'd learned enough English for the first encounter. As usual, we had to talk about our ages and education, our emigration to Israel, our time in France, and our plans for Canada, knowing full well that they already had the answers and were really just trying to form an impression of our personalities.

It took us about a week to do all the medical tests needed and to fill out the various documents, after which we needed to pick up our immigration papers from the Canadian embassy. We had two weeks to wrap up our affairs in Paris and buy tickets to Toronto. We sold whatever we could, left the rest to our Israeli friends, and prepared bank drafts for the money we'd saved over our three years in France.

Canada

We arrived at Toronto Pearson International Airport on October 18, 1978. It was already cold there, but fortunately we had warm clothes with us. We couldn't walk out of the airport right away as we had to go through immigration. It took us about two hours—and Abrasha and Zina calling the immigration officer from the arrival area—until we were allowed out.

Our new friends took us to their home, gave us a large room in the basement, and helped us during our first days in Canada. Two days after our arrival, I visited Chabad to discuss the particulars of my job with two rabbis. Unfortunately, the organization had changed its plans: the number of newcomers wasn't growing as forecast and attention had shifted to bringing newcomer Soviet Jews into the faith—for which they needed a Russian-speaking rabbi. They advised me to look for other work options. I thanked them for bringing me to Canada, left them the gifts I had brought them from France, and started thinking about what to do.

I wondered if any of my past friends lived in Toronto. One day I looked through the telephone directory and saw a familiar first-last name combination, Vladimir M. I called; and the person on the receiving end responded in Russian. It was Vladimir M. whom I had lent money to in Moscow and later run into in Jerusalem! He'd been in Canada for more than four years, was married, and had a little daughter. He invited us to his apartment and was very happy to see us. As we exchanged our life experiences, I told him the history of my association with the Chabad organization, the long process of coming to Canada, and my current struggle finding a job. He told me that he'd applied for the exact same position at Chabad too and that this had strangely, but obviously, contributed to the delay of my immigration. Once again, our lives continued to collide in improbable ways. We maintained a good relationship with Vladimir and his family for many years in Canada.

After a lot of unsuccessful interviews, I landed a job at Northern Telecom. Thankfully, they were looking for programmers. Like many other companies, they had moved their head office from Montreal to Toronto because of the political unrest in Quebec and were hiring anyone who knew Cobol. After a very simple interview and test, I was offered a job (for which I was overqualified) with a salary of eighteen thousand dollars a year. I was told that there were formalities that would take about two weeks until I could start.

A few days later, I received a phone call from my new friend Leonid (Vladimir had made the connection). Leonid had helped me prepare my Canadian résumé; he asked if I had already found a job. He said that—despite some job insecurity at his company—he had an offer for me. Besides running his own business (translating and writing résumés), Leonid worked in sales at Pertec, which manufactured minicomputers in California and had sales offices in the United States and Canada. Leonid had shown my résumé to his boss, and he was ready to hire me based on Leonid's reference. After meeting Leonid's boss, I secured my first job in Canada as a system programmer with a twenty thousand dollar a year salary. I thought that the job involved developing and improving the operating system of minicomputers. I thus expected to be taught to do that while, in parallel, providing technical support for sales.

A week after I was hired, I was sent for training to the Los Angeles head office. It was the end of January, cold and snowy in Toronto, when I left Fania and Karine alone for three weeks. Abrasha and Zina promised to help Fania if needed so I could fly to LA. As it turned out, however, my time there was less than satisfying. Despite staying on an additional week—which didn't impress Fania—and having no time to get any sense of California, I discovered that the job would be more focused on sales support and less on actual programming. I returned to Toronto to find little work, a bleak atmosphere, and greater job insecurity. Leonid came to me with the bad news that, since the Toronto office hadn't made its sales targets, he would be let go in a day or two and I would most likely be laid off a few days later. It wasn't a shock, considering what was going on at the company, but it certainly pushed me to plan ahead.

That same day I called HR at Northern Telecom and asked them what had happened with the result of my interview about six weeks earlier. I was told that my file was with them and it looked good, but they hadn't been able to connect with me. Since I was still interested in the job, I took a half day off from Pertec, filled out paperwork, and accepted a job as a Cobol programmer at Northern Telecom—a company with more than twenty thousand employees across Canada. My starting salary at NT was twenty-one thousand dollars a year. The next day I resigned from Pertec.

After ten years at Northern Telecom, I was considering retiring to start my own consulting business.[5] I had turned down an opportunity to be transferred to Miami, as well as other internal opportunities, and thankfully had listened to my intuition (Northern Telecom would soon go famously bankrupt). However, the Royal Bank of Canada asked me to join a few specialists in a very lucrative position in its IT architecture group. The offer intrigued me. It took many weeks of negotiations—I insisted on a higher base salary and better benefits before I would alter my plans to become a consultant; the company met my terms and I agreed to join RBC as it made the transition to electronic banking. Meanwhile, the day after my ten-year anniversary at NT, I resigned from my position, but then discovered that in my ten years of service I had accumulated only twenty-five thousand dollars in my pension fund—less than half a year's salary. Nevertheless, getting in on the ground floor of a new wave of technology was exciting, there was job security, and, despite some struggles as the team staff arrived at a consensus on how we would work together, I was happy in my new job at RBC.

I had spent fourteen years at the bank in the IT and risk management departments when my routine work was interrupted by an unusual request from my boss: he wanted me to check the pricing of our bank's mortgage-backed securities. An MBS is an asset-backed security issued by a company created by a bank. The company manages a bundle of mortgages from the bank's portfolio and issues MBS (mortgage-backed securities). Our bank had an office in New York dealing with this and my task was to ensure that its pricing for MBSs was accurate. It seemed like an interesting new area, so I enthusiastically agreed to take on the project.

Unfortunately, it didn't work out as I wanted: I was only able to obtain the ratings calculated by outside agencies. To check the accuracy of the rates, I needed to see more detailed information on every MBS. Despite my efforts, I couldn't obtain the information, but the company insisted that I complete the task using the secondary numbers. Ultimately, I told my boss that I wouldn't do it because: (a) the work could be completed by any undergraduate financial math student, and (b) the task I was being asked to do,

---

5   During this time, like many immigrants, I had side hustles that were less than glamorous. For example, my boss would hire me on the sly to help out with his weekend house-flipping endeavors, work that included digging trenches for stone fences and porches, painting basements, and other physical tasks, for three dollars per hour. I did it on the weekends for many years.

without the source information, reminded me of the USSR, where managers almost always gave their subordinates challenging assignments and then forced them to sign project documents which would make them a scapegoat when things went wrong. I told my boss that I felt that I was being set up, and I thought that I should resign. Fania, as always, supported my decision to take early retirement, reminding me that we only live once. My decision to retire saved me from a potentially difficult situation when the global financial crisis struck a few years later.

Family

Meanwhile, life at home kept evolving. After living in a small apartment at Roselawn and Eglinton, Fania and I were able to purchase our first Toronto house in 1980. And in the summer of 1981, Fania became pregnant with our second child—a son, Alan—who was born after a difficult pregnancy that hospitalized her for the last two months and concluded with a cesarean section. We were thrilled to have a son; however, Fania needed more attention and my help for a while.

Despite the vast distance between Toronto and Frunze, Fania was very connected to her mother; they spoke at least once a month on the phone. In June 1985, Fania received a telegram from her middle brother Roma in Frunze that her mother had had a stroke and was in the hospital in a serious condition. Fania's first impulse was to fly to Frunze to be at her mother's bedside, but she needed to obtain a visa from the Soviet embassy in Ottawa. As she was under severe stress, I called the embassy and eventually managed to talk to a Russian receptionist. She took our information and left me waiting. Fifteen minutes later, she came back to the phone and told me the visa had been denied; but she couldn't tell me why. I insisted on talking to the person who had made the decision and, after putting some pressure on the receptionist, she transferred me to the man in charge. I asked him to explain why Fania couldn't see her very sick, and possibly dying, mother. He told me that the Soviet embassy in Ottawa had information about how Fania had left the Soviet Union, and that she understood that she'd never be allowed back. I tried to argue that this was inhumane. But he kept repeating: you knew the consequences of your actions when you left the USSR, so don't complain. Finally, I called him a pig and slammed the phone down. Three days later Roma called us from Frunze to tell us that their mother had passed away. Rabbi Lipsker and his wife visited us while Fania was sitting shiva.

In 1988 we decided that we needed more space, so we sold our semi-detached house. I happened upon a model home, which was almost double the amount that we'd planned to spend, and insisted that Fania look at it. She fell in love with it and wanted to buy it. Here our friends, Zina and Abrasha, again set us in the right direction. They counseled us "not to live our lives with a calculator in our hands": we should get what we wanted and needed; life would lead us into a new reality where we'd learn to live by adjusting ourselves and seizing new opportunities. They reminded us that, ten years earlier, we'd been uncertain about surviving and thriving in Canada; now, in 1988, we were pretty much settled and we were both still young and energetic and able to continue to grow. They were right. We experienced many family milestones in that home, including welcoming Fania's brothers to stay with us for a while after we sponsored them to emigrate to Canada when the Iron Curtain fell and inviting my sister Hanna and her family to join us from Israel.

While this chapter is about Canada, I had a strange, unnerving (and unexpected) run-in with Soviet culture in 1990. My boss proposed that I take a paid vacation with my family and do some reading for an upcoming project. It was wintertime and the most affordable, warm, and nearby option at the time was Cuba—but the country had only recently opened itself to tourism. Our travel agent assured us that it would be a safe option, despite our background; Cuba had been under economic control by Moscow for quite some time, but that support was beginning to wane. While I didn't really think of it at the time (though I should probably have considered it), it turned out that we were one of the first, if not the first, ex-Soviets vacationing in Cuba, and it caused a little stir upon our arrival.

Our flight to Cuba from Toronto was on an old Soviet-built airplane—a Tupolev Tu-104—and the passenger pamphlets were written in Russian. As we arrived at the Cuban customs desk and presented our passports, the officer—a man with a long mustache and an unfriendly disposition—could not understand the birthplaces marked in our passports, considering we had just arrived from Canada. In my passport, my birthplace was UZB and in Fania's it was KGZ. After we explained that Uzbekistan and Kyrgyzstan were in the Soviet Union, his eyebrows arched in surprise. He slipped away into a room behind his passport control desk for a long, long while. Fania and I began to get quite nervous—all the terrible old memories of escaping Russia flooded our minds. We were in a predicament: we had willingly, yet unwittingly, placed ourselves at the mercy of Russia's allies. Would they detain us? Question us? Throw us in a Cuban prison? However many tens of minutes it took for the man to return it certainly felt like many hours.

When the officer finally returned, he would not meet our gaze and simply stamped our passports; we were permitted to enter Cuba, but it certainly didn't feel like a cheery welcome. Later during the trip we met many lovely Cubans (most of whom spoke fluent Russian, as it was a mandatory subject at school) and fellow Canadian vacationers. We had a nice time. The small slice of Cuba we saw was beautiful, of course. But there were various moments when we experienced the familiar Soviet vibe: in the dining hall where waitresses could not bring an additional napkin to the table without a manager's approval (they were counted carefully, along with the cutlery, and doled out sparingly); or at the hotel lobby bar where the bartender was actually an electrical engineer. He worked evenings mixing drinks for tourists because his government salary and the *Libreta* food and grocery rationing didn't cover his family's needs. Tourist tips were essential for buying necessities on the black market.

I overheard some Russian-speaking people who walked past us on the beach discuss Cuban rum. I decided to walk behind them, at a distance, out of curiosity. They were Soviet citizens who were permitted by the KGB to spend time in Cuba for their contributions to Russia. When I went further along the same beach another day I came to a beachfront building that was surrounded by a very tall barbed wire fence festooned with "No Trespassing" signs. There were armed Cuban security guards around it—and they less-than-gently suggested I turn around and head back to my hotel. I later learned from Cuban waiters I had befriended at our hotel that I had come across a "resort" for Soviet astronauts and that nobody was allowed anywhere near the fence, let alone the building. Our Cuban vacation was tropical and warm, but more importantly it was useful: it made me realize how relieved I was that I didn't live anywhere like the Soviet Union.

Fania decided to get a job in Canada around this time. She had worked in a Russian bakery and had done some at-home childcare, but she was now ready to build a career. She applied for an assistant teacher position at Bialik Hebrew Day School, given that she had a solid teaching record in Israel and kindergarten experience in France. She registered Alan for the first grade at Bialik, as this was the most convenient arrangement for all of us. He was a bright child (he read encyclopedias, scientific magazines, fiction, and news-papers from second grade onward) and also very social: he could easily talk with people of any age. Growing up in Bialik had instilled in him a strong relationship with his Jewish faith.

When Alan was twelve, I wanted him to switch to an independent school for students in Grades 7 to 12, affiliated with University of Toronto called University of Toronto Schools (UTS); they had enriched curricu-lums, but it meant giving up his Hebrew and Torah studies. We struck a deal: he would continue his schooling at UTS and I would attend synagogue with him on Saturdays and join him in studying Torah. Thus, Alan became one of the only Jewish boys at his school and the only one who wore a yar-mulke (religious head covering) on his head. He didn't care: he was making a statement!

After Alan's bar mitzvah we took a family trip: we went to London, Paris, and then Israel. We stayed with my mom in Petah Tikva and then traveled up north to Kibbutz Eilon, where my brother was musical director of Keshet Eilon International Master Courses for talented young violinists. We visited Jerusalem several times—the Old City and the Western Wall. Having been away for twenty years, my impression of Israel in 1995 was that the country had become wealthier: there were beautiful new highways and new houses in many towns that looked like well-kept villas.

Alan was a good negotiator; each time we would press him to do some-thing, he secured good conditions for his "surrender." When he agreed to apply to the engineering program at the University of Toronto, he asked to take a year off to spend time at a yeshiva in Israel. He chose to apply to a yeshiva in a kibbutz on Mount Gilboa. We visited him there in the fall and enjoyed a few days in the kibbutz and surrounding places.

Alan grew into an impressive young man: he earned a bachelor in mechanical engineering and an MBA in 2007. Ultimately, he married and relocated to Israel, where he got divorced but thrived at work. But he died suddenly in his Israeli apartment in June 2011. Shocked by the news, Fania, Karine, and I decided to bring Alan to Toronto for burial. His death changed the family dynamic; things were never quite the same afterwards.

Reuven's son Alan on the Niagara River.

Brain Power

Like her brother, Karine did well at school, and she was quite musical and artistically talented; however, by the time she was in third or fourth grade, I became dissatisfied with the quality of her school's math program. I decided that a few times a week I would give her some personalized math enrichment by teaching her problem-solving and logical thinking skills. That said, learning together was very difficult for the two of us. Teaching your own child is not the same as teaching at school; I considered starting a small class. Pursuing this option required me to revise the material I had from Jerusalem and Paris—a process which took more than a year.

When I had finally assembled enough material to start running a program, I approached neighbors who had kids about Karine's age and invited their children to attend my class twice a week in the evenings, for free; it would be "edu-tainment" in our basement. I used a white Formica cabinet from our old kitchen for a blackboard (the whiteboard markers worked surprisingly well on it!). The kids sat on the carpet and we played many interesting logic games, learned math, and solved problems. Slowly these classes became very popular, and the first groups of parents were so grateful for my work that they began telling their friends to join me, too.

In late spring, before school ended for the summer, I announced that we would conclude our studies. In mid-June, some parents knocked at the door. They brought me a gift—a twenty-five-volume *Encyclopedia Britannica*—and begged me to continue the classes in the next school year, offering to pay me. No matter how many times I told them that I didn't have anything prepared, they'd repeat that their kids had really enjoyed themselves and had learned a huge amount. We must continue, they said. Eventually, I relented: I calculated what I could charge by consulting with informed friends and considering what it would take to spend the summer getting ready. It turned out to be about one-third of what parents would pay for private tutoring; so I set about making a curriculum for the next academic year. To my surprise, my free school would grow into an educational enterprise called Brain Power.

By September of 1989, I pretty much had two jobs: one at Northern Telecom and another out of our home. I started buying books with logic problems, mazes, and engaging math questions (whatever I could find in bookstores) and used these in my teaching. I also found that I was avoiding (as much as possible) any projects at NT that required more than two or three days away from home so I could keep my commitments to my students.

By that time, I was teaching twice a week, with seven or eight students sitting on the floor of our mostly unfinished basement. It was okay for now, but we soon realized that this setup was neither sustainable nor convenient. Fania and I started looking into building a proper classroom in the basement. However, this idea wasn't really workable: we would need to partition the basement, put up walls, and carpet the concrete floor—work I couldn't do myself because I lacked both the time and skills. We got a few estimates from contractors, but they were absolutely beyond our reach. I was then introduced to a Jamaican contractor, who was eager to get the job. After he made some measurements, quickly drew up a layout (allowing me a large classroom, an office, a small bedroom, and a shower room with toilet) and quoted only twelve thousand dollars, I hired him on the spot.

He did an excellent job, but he found that he had underestimated the work and would need several thousand dollars more to complete the task. Since that extra cost was more than we could afford, I paid him for all that he'd done and we parted ways. After that, we finished it ourselves and bought some of the basics we would need to operate the program. Brain Power moved to the "new" basement. With the money I'd saved from teaching, I was able to put down fresh carpet, get a few more desks, and buy a ping-pong table. This allowed me to accommodate daily classes in the basement and the growing number of students. In time, I started to develop classes for new age groups.

When Karine was in sixth grade, I noticed her doing an unusual math project: she was to clip coupons from newspapers and glue these to a bristol board until there was one hundred dollars in total. I was distraught about this, so I met with the school principal. I showed him what the kids were doing and what kind of homework they were getting. When he asked what I expected, I reminded him that he'd promised that his school offered special programs for bright and gifted kids (indeed, Karine had sat an exam to qualify for the program). I asked him why kids in sixth grade were doing second-grade work. To my disappointment, I learned that Karine's math teacher was really a dance teacher; she was trying to integrate "artistic skills" into mathematics. However, I suspect that neither art nor math was being properly addressed.

Unable to hold back, I exploded. I told him about my teaching experiences in the USSR, Israel, and France; I told him about Brain Power, offered him my material for fifth through eighth grades for free use in his school; and I even offered to teach the teachers in his school some useful methods of delivering math to bright and gifted kids. Perhaps my less-than-gentle approach wasn't ideal, but my message was received. The principal sent me to get the school board's approval to use my materials. I spent a month preparing, made a presentation, and discovered—after a lot of red tape and terrible trouble with the teachers' union—that my plans would never be accepted. In fact, at my presentation, someone sarcastically asked something along the lines of, "If you think the Soviet education system's so good, why did you move to Canada?" I withdrew my offer immediately. Ultimately, I did get a letter of eligibility to teach from the board, but I never used it. I hung it on my wall as a reminder of the resistance I met with when trying to work within the system.

One night after she got home from work, Fania told me that the principal at Bialik Hebrew Day School was interested in Brain Power and would like to talk to me. When we met, he offered to let me run two after-school classes for six months. I accepted the offer. Twice a week, I left the bank earlier to be at Bialik by five o'clock. The students in my classes were bright and engaged, and we enjoyed ourselves. Because of this exposure, I started getting more new students for Brain Power at home.

Just before the winter holidays, I got a phone call at work from someone representing Vaughan City Hall (we lived in Thornhill, which was part of Vaughan). The caller asked if I was running a school at home; he'd had complaints from one of our neighbors, who'd said there was increased traffic on our street, parents waiting on our lawn, and a large number of youngsters coming and going. Sheepish, I could not deny the allegation, and offered to have cars park and parents wait elsewhere; I was ordered to shut down my school.

I announced to my students and their parents that the program was suspended until further notice; but one parent called me with a temporary solution. She was willing to let us use the meeting room at the back of her business for our classes. The move left me with a grueling schedule: five days a week, I would leave home at 6:45 a.m. to be at work for about 8:15; I would leave work at 5:00 pm to be in class by 6:30 pm; and I would get home at around 10:00 p.m. But registrations for my classes went up after changing to the new location.

After six months, a unit became available near the business unit—and in the same strip mall in north Toronto. I took it, and we moved into a facility with two classrooms and a storage room. During the summer, I built shelving in the storage room to keep and manage my classroom material. The fall Brain Power classes filled up, and I needed help to run classes. Karine had assisted me when it was in our home, once she'd completed high school. She started working part-time at Brain Power in its new location, then, so I could cope with the growing number of students.

Karine finished her undergraduate degrees concurrently—a bachelor of science (hons) and a bachelor of education. One of her professors believed that she had enormous talent and a sharp mind and nudged her to pursue a master's degree in education. She thus completed a master's from the Ontario Institute for Studies in Education at the University of Toronto and then started her PhD in 2006. I was pleased, as I saw that she had unique pedagogical abilities, she connected with students and parents with much warmth and ease, and she was on her way to building a very nice career. Moreover, Karine was incredibly driven—helping people was her passion and her work ethic was second to none.

Karine's PhD graduation, 2010.

Eventually, an even larger unit became vacant on our floor: we leased it and hired contractors to convert the unit into three large classrooms and two offices—one for me and one for Karine. By that time, Karine had completed a year of private teaching with the Reichmann family. She'd developed an excellent junior high language arts program for one of their children and she was excited to expand it and introduce it to small groups of students. I thought that mathematics was far more in demand and tried to dissuade her from this direction. She insisted, of course, and I watched her program flourish. With our larger space, the student body also increased, and I started earning almost as much at Brain Power as at the Royal Bank of Canada. But working in two places, sometimes fifteen to sixteen hours a day, became difficult.

With Karine's help, I had more time to think about the future of the school. I realized that my math program needed a more formal approach. People liked my math and problem-solving classes, and the number of students grew every year without any advertising. I decided that I needed to write books that would support in-class teaching and provide homework assignments. My vision was to develop student workbooks to emphasize thinking skills (analytical and creative thinking, memory development, math skills, and problem-solving strategies and methods). I finished the first draft of my first book in 2003, but I learned that big publishers wouldn't touch a manuscript that hadn't come through a publishing agent and hadn't been rigorously edited. The parent of one of my students helped me out yet again, though: she directed me to AuthorHouse. After much work, Karine and I put out two volumes (student and teacher versions of *Brain Power Enrichment, Level One, Book One*) under their auspices in 2007.

Almost immediately, it became clear that I needed to publish workbooks and teachers' manuals for the second term of level one (fourth to sixth grade) and to expand the resources for older students. Between 2007 and 2018, we wrote books for levels two (sixth to eighth grade), three (eighth to tenth grade), four (eighth to eleventh grade), and five (ninth to twelfth grade).

As I continued to write and publish, Karine developed and expanded her language arts programs, included a new public speaking program that was immediately in high demand, and created other sought-after enrichment offerings. We had waiting lists, some very high-profile families had enrolled, and all the while we ensured that students in financial need would still be able to learn with us. It was word-of-mouth and organic growth. She began hiring other talented PhD educators to join her team and created an ideal learning community for bright and talented youth. Karine's lineup of courses gave students and parents numerous options, and my own work at Brain Power expanded. I had hundreds of students every year, which gave me more administrative work—refining my registration practices, developing financial-control packages, and managing my staff. Karine's side of the program was much larger, growing even faster, and she handled it all with aplomb.

Over time, Karine and I disagreed about the business more and more. She was keen on ensuring quality control and same-standard experiences as the organization grew. She was also intent on integrating technology (bringing in a Learning Management System, a Customer Relationship Management System, various payment options, etc.). Karine transformed the branding, worked on our website, and also dedicated herself to creating out-of-class learning experiences for our students (field trips, competitions, community events and more). Meanwhile, I was set on keeping things flexible in the math department and staying true to more traditional methods of running classes, dealing with clients, and running registration (I was often accused of being "old-fashioned"). I wanted each of my math teachers to adapt to each of their groups and work closely with me to ensure excellence. Of course, Karine was worried that the math program would remain small or even collapse if something happened to me. She wanted to have programs that could run without either of us. Her team and her success grew. For some time, we basically rented the same space but had separate businesses - and we often butted heads. I watched Karine expand her excellent programs to include bright students in first through twelfth grades and her business became very popular, gained much recognition, and gave back to the community. I am proud to say that one part of her language arts curriculum could trace its lineage to my youth in the Soviet Union. I had introduced Karine to Isaak Babel's *Odessa Stories*, which I had first encountered in my friend Vova's apartment when I was a schoolboy and later received from Anatoly Glance when I was in the Red Army. Karine read the book in English translation and fell in love with it. When she developed her high school language arts curriculum, she crafted a "Classic Russian Literature" syllabus to showcase Russian writers who had influenced story-telling across the globe. She'd inserted Babel's stories at the end to give the students a feel for a voice that was different from Tolstoy, Dostoevsky, and the other classics. As far as I know, to this day Brain Power still showcases Babel and students still respond well to his storytelling.

As the number of students grew, we again needed more space, and again had to move. We spent more than two years looking. Exhausted, we turned to a real estate agent for help. In a few months, Karine found a beautiful place in a newly built Jewish community center: there was a sizable unoccupied space on the third floor, the rest of which was occupied by various medical specialists. The building was classy and situated in a new neighborhood which had lots of families with kids who could be interested in our programs.

To check things out, we leased two rooms on the second floor and ran some math and language arts classes. It was great, but the rent was very high. Karine was keen, but I was reluctant. I only agreed to the lease if it was in her name only. This is when Karine met her new landlord, David Sadowski (mentioned in Chapter 5).

It was an empty shell of a bit more than 2,500 square feet. Karine had to hire an architect to design the facility with five large classrooms, an office for administrative personnel, and meeting and storage rooms. The construction was costly and took many months to complete. Before moving in, Karine decided to create a unique construction project: she would make the school a model for progressive enrichment education. The physical space would be one that the kids would both learn in and from. She hired a minority woman-led construction team, only used recycled or green products (for example, the walls were made out of recycled pressed juice boxes, the insulation was made from recycled jeans, etc.), and involved interested students in upcycling materials with which to create a giant sixteen-foot brain mural (this went on to win an award from Canada's Green Building Council in 2014).

Because our project was so innovative, it drew a lot of attention from the community. There was a grand opening night celebration, complete with city dignitaries cutting the ribbon. The CEO of York Region presided over the event, and members of Parliament and the mayor gave speeches about how happy they were that we had chosen to bring our educational expertise to the children of the City of Vaughan. There also were many students and parents present.

It was an excellent move for us: in our first year, enrolment grew by 30 percent. We hired more instructors and began operating six days a week. Fania took a sabbatical from her kindergarten to help us in our office (and because working with young children while mourning the death of Alan was too difficult for her); then, a year later, she decided to retire from her kindergarten job to join us at Brain Power full time.

After some medical issues and a serious operation, I came to realize that I no longer had the physical strength to teach two-hour lessons; they were too hard on my body and soul. It was the end of my working life. After a long and serious conversation with Fania and Karine, I decided to retire and left my Brain Power math program to Karine: it was now hers. She finally had the freedom to take Brain Power to the next level.

Her team grew to more than forty employees and consultants—many of them PhDs—and she won a lot of awards as an entrepreneur (in the City of Vaughan, the Greater Toronto Area, and all of Canada). She also received accolades as a woman in business and even received the prestigious Order of Vaughan Award from the mayor, something only given to individuals who have made a major impact on the city. Her contributions to education and ability to draw talent to Brain Power from all across the province were recognized at a beautiful ceremony. The school's alumni were now in the thousands, and many of these bright young people were becoming impressive leaders in their respective careers and attributing their success to us. Karine's next steps to further grow Brain Power began in 2021, when she opened up a successful new location in Hamilton, Ontario at McMaster University's Innovation Park. The following year, she brought in a CEO from UofT's Rotman School of Management, and began making plans to expand across Canada.

Returning "Home"

In the summer of 2008, while we were visiting Alan in Israel, I received a phone call from Sasha Svirsky, my good friend from my Odesa days. We hadn't spoken since my immigration to Israel in 1971 (it was impossible to do so during the Soviet period). He invited me to Odesa for a reunion with a small number of our university friends, and promised to provide me with accommodation in one of his apartments. I agreed hesitantly, and Fania and I took a plane from Israel to Odesa. Sasha met us at the airport, and we spent ten days in the city of my youth (which was filled with pleasant and not-so-pleasant memories).

I was very saddened to see how decrepit the math faculty building had become: pieces of the parquet had torn away; student desks were broken; and the professors' doors bore the same scratches they'd had forty years before. I was astonished to see that the area on the second floor where the university's mainframe computer was located was surrounded by a barbed wire fence to protect against thieves. Since it was mid-July, there were not many students on campus.

We also visited the famous, and newly renovated, Opera House. The inside of the building was opulent, but the *Carmen* we went to see was amateurish; we left during the intermission. In general, I was depressed there because it wasn't the same city I had left in 1971. All the streets had been restored to their prerevolution names and people on the street mainly spoke Ukrainian without the Odesa accent.

While Fania and I were at my classmate Irina's apartment with fifteen of my former university friends, reminiscing and drinking, everyone complained about their miserable lives after the collapse of the Soviet Union. Most of my old friends were PhDs teaching at universities or other institutes of higher education. During the 1990s, faculty were paid not in money but in chinaware, which they sold at a flea market to get some cash. Irina told me that, in addition to financial difficulties, Odesa had experienced a lack of good physicians and engineers. When asked where these professionals had gone, Irina said that they were in Israel, Brighton Beach, and other "good" places. After drinking some whiskey and eating cookies, Fania and I said our goodbyes.

The following day, we took a taxi from the Odesa railroad station to Belgorod-Dnestrovsky to visit the places of my childhood. It was a two-hour drive past the lovely sandy beaches of Karolino-Bugaz and Bugaz on the Black Sea and the village of Shabo where my father had been born. Finally, we arrived at the railroad station in Belgorod-Dnestrovsky. It was a sweltering day—more than 95°F. The station's square was almost empty except for a few taxis and a few drunk people sitting on old benches. We started walking toward the city center; the streets were empty; the same old one-story multifamily buildings framed each side of the street; cobblestones were missing from the road; and the sidewalks were so filled with cracks and holes that it was dangerous to walk without looking down.

The central farmers' market was closed that day, but two or three rows of kiosks and tables under umbrellas stood on its perimeter. It was like a flea market with lots of sellers and almost no buyers. We went to see the building where my family had lived at the end of the 1940s. The apartment building wasn't there; instead, there was a shiny automobile dealership building on the lot. I took Fania to the building where my paternal grandmother had lived, but I almost missed it because a two-story multifamily building had replaced the synagogue that had been next door.

From there, we walked up to Victory Park. Because of the heat, we stopped at the park's café to buy ice cream and water. We passed the restaurant where my dad used to play drums in the evenings; in its place we saw a boarded-up, abandoned restaurant. After that, we passed by the new City Hall that had been built after my time there and visited my childhood school; we walked into the empty backyard and around the building. It was closed, so we continued to the fortress built by the Ottomans on the banks of the Dniester River about six hundred years ago. We noticed that some restoration had been done to the walls and towers and an open-air restaurant inside the fortress.

We walked to my old house; the building hadn't been looked after since we'd left in the 1970s; the tall tree in the backyard was gone; and there was a long shallow trench housing a water pipe (recently installed so that people could fill their pails with drinking water in their own backyards rather than having to walk 150 yards). The kitchen wall that my father had built atop an entrance to the building's cellar was no longer straight. The old outhouse was still there, but it was covered with rotten, greyed wood and metal sheets; the small flowerbeds contained tomato plants that had dried under the scorching sun; there were old, yellowed drapes in the windows; and no people were about.

I walked a few steps up to see what was going on in our old apartment when the door opened, and a woman, about sixty years old, stepped out and asked what I was looking for there. I told her that my family had lived there many years ago and I was visiting from abroad. She looked at me and asked if I was the son of Gregory who owned this place in the 1970s. I said yes and we had a short conversation. She never invited us inside. She complained about how difficult life was for the town's people: the local government failed to maintain the town; there was a serious lack of employment, and their lives were miserable. When I asked her about my former neighbors, she gave me sad news: a few people had died; some were sick; and some had moved out. My friend's father, Ivan Ivanovich Ivanov, had died many years before; his wife Nataly still lived in their apartment; however, on that particular day, she happened to be visiting her children, who lived about twenty minutes walking distance away. She gave me the address for Nataly's family, and Fania and I went there.

The Ivanov family was waiting for us when we showed up. The woman we'd met before had called Nataly to tell her that we were coming. All of them were sitting in the backyard around a long table in the shade of a gigantic tree.

Fania's face was red from the heat of the sun, and she didn't feel well. They took her inside to wash her face with cold water. After initial hugs, tears, and introductions, we heard some Ivanov family stories. After her husband, Ivan Ivanovich Ivanov, had died, Nataly became more active in her religious community, the Seventh Day Adventists. She suffered a lot because of her affiliation with the religious group; her husband, a member of the Communist Party, was often reprimanded for having a religious wife; he had beaten her after each party meeting and whenever he was drunk, which happened with increasing frequency.

After his death, and after the collapse of the regime, Nataly became a Church leader, a very respected and loved person. There was a spirit and aura about her; she looked very different from when we'd been neighbors. She asked me about my parents, brothers, and sisters, and asked me to send love to my mom. She remembered how my mom had helped her avoid violence from her husband, given her food, and welcomed her to our home to discuss the Bible.

The home where we met belonged to her youngest son, Ivan. He was a young, tall, and handsome guy, but he was reticent and hardly said a word. Nataly explained that he'd had an accident when serving in the army; his truck had overturned and he'd been left with a severe brain injury. Ivan's wife sat at the table, hardly talking. Then Nataly's daughter Larissa showed up full of energy and smiles. I remembered her as a little girl with a runny nose, crying, and asking for candies. She was now a strong and articulate middle-aged woman. She invited me to come and see her house, which was about a block away. As we walked, we passed the fish factory where my mom had worked for more than twenty-five years; it had been closed, but someone had bought the equipment and was producing canned fish for Ukrainian prisons. We also passed a once-popular communal bathhouse; it was now a brothel. Larissa's one-story house had a backyard bursting with flowerbeds full of southern flowers and shrubs. Her husband was home watching television and uninterested in guests.

When we returned to her brother's home, I asked Nataly about her oldest son, my friend Vitaly. She picked up a telephone, dialed, and passed it to me. He was on the other end. I got a spasm in my throat when I heard his voice. I had neither seen nor talked to my friend for about forty years, and the emotion overcame me. After gulping a bit of water, I could speak. He was in another city, near Rostov-on-Don, but he wanted to see Fania and me, so we agreed to meet him at 9:00 a.m. the next day in front of Odesa's railroad station. After our conversation, Fania and I called a taxi to go to the Belgorod-Dnestrovsky station. From there, we shared a taxi van to Odesa with eight other people.

The next morning, Fania and I stood in front of Odesa's station waiting for Vitaly. At 9:30, as I was pacing back and forth looking at the traffic and people, I saw a strange guy in tight shorts and a bright yellow t-shirt walking toward Fania with a single red rose in his hand. I went over and said that we hadn't ordered any flowers. He looked at me, started laughing, and told me that he was Vitaly. Tears were in my eyes as we hugged. He had driven the whole night to get there; his wife was asleep in his car; and he didn't want to disturb her. We agreed to meet in three days, on Monday, at the same place. He departed that morning for Belgorod-Dnestrovsky to rest, see his family, and prepare for our get-together.

Fania and I wanted to look around Odesa and see what Jewish life was like there now. We were advised to visit a new Chabad synagogue that had been restored on Kanatnaia Street. The communist regime had confiscated the building and the land in the 1930s; it had been a store, a warehouse, and after World War II it had been abandoned in ruins. The city authorities returned it, along with a few other places, to the remnants of the Jewish community after the collapse of communism. Chabad had built a beautiful synagogue on the land—a place frequently visited by foreign travelers. We were there in the morning, and a large group of English-speaking Jews (about fifty people) walked in. The English-speaking rabbi gave a presentation about the Jewish community of Odesa. He talked about how the community of 250,000 Jews in the 1970s had shrunk to only 35,000 in 2008; how many synagogues there were; how many Jewish schools and centers existed now; and how other things had changed over the years. The rabbi also suggested visiting a nearby kosher restaurant affiliated with the synagogue, so we went there for lunch after the presentation.

It was a beautiful, clean place with white tablecloths and a menu that included traditional Jewish food, like cholent, soups, fish, and other delights. I spoke with the restaurant owner, a young Chabad Orthodox man who was planning to travel to North America, and answered his questions about Jewish life in Toronto and Canada. A group of four Americans sat at a table near ours; I greeted them, we exchanged pleasantries, and they asked me how Jews in Canada saw the possibility of Barack Obama being elected to the US presidency. I told them that it was difficult to talk about the Jewish community as a whole in Canada, but that I thought that Obama would likely be less than favorable for the United States, Israel, and Jews worldwide. They were taken aback, and ultimately called me a racist, a man with a limited vision. The Americans were clearly Jewish liberals from New Jersey. I stopped talking with them, we finished eating, and left.

The next day we went to the Odesa port by going down the famous Potemkin Stairs. As we walked along the pier, about thirty young religious Jewish girls speaking Yiddish passed by us. Then we took a cable car up and walked to Odesa City Hall. I wanted Fania to see the OVIR building where, in 1971, I'd finally gotten permission to leave the USSR. The building was now the city police headquarters; a guard stood in front and police officers hurried in and out. The guard didn't allow me to go inside the building, and he became angry when I asked for a photo of me and him. He ordered me to go.

We walked up back to the Central Synagogue of Odesa, which was housed in a building that had been a library in the 1970s. We wanted to look inside, but a young security guard with a gun stopped us, saying that today, on Friday, the public wasn't allowed in until about 7:00 p.m., when the Sabbath prayers started. After explaining to him that we were from Canada and couldn't wait until then, I said I would like to have about ten or fifteen minutes for an early *mincha* (afternoon) prayer. We negotiated a little, and he eventually let me into the first floor and Fania to the balcony on the second floor. It was dark inside; the only light was in front of the cabinet where the Torah scrolls were kept. I read my prayer and we walked out. I noticed a pizzeria across the street and a kosher restaurant in the synagogue's backyard. A few young Jewish Orthodox boys passed by us on the street. That was the new Odesa—so different from my time, from the 1960s and 1970s.

On Sunday, we invited Sasha and his wife to a nice restaurant near them that overlooked the Black Sea's beach. And, finally, on Monday, we saw Vitaly and spent half a day with him, walking and reminiscing, talking about our kids, work, and achievements, and sharing our losses. We ate lunch in the restaurant adjacent to the Central Synagogue, and Vitaly promised to come to the airport to say goodbye before we departed for Israel.

It was a rainy day, and Sasha couldn't take us to the airport. Instead, he asked one of our university classmates, Yuri Matveev, to drive us. When we arrived, Yuri gave me a few books about the city, including a cookbook. We've used it for many years now. Vitaly arrived at the airport with his daughter, my sister Hanna's childhood friend, and a former classmate. We only had ten minutes to hug each other and say our goodbyes before boarding the plane.

My return to Odesa left me with bittersweet memories and sorrow at the state of my childhood home. And the sorrow continues. The places where I spent my youth have been engulfed in the war that Russia launched against Ukraine in 2022. As this book was being completed, I happened to see on the television news that an airbase in Crimea had been hit—the same airbase where I did my army service. In that part of the world—a place from which I was so happy to escape—the suffering has not ended.

Photographs

Reuven (left) and Vova, 1958.

Reuven's first month of military service, November 1964.

Reuven and his brothers, 1967: Fima (left), Izia (middle), Reuven (right).

Reuven with Djilda, "Uncle" Sasha's dog, 1970.

"Uncle" Sasha Ovsianikov with Djilda and her puppy, 1970.

Reuven (far left) and his classmates skipping a Theory of Numbers university lecture to drink beer near Deribasovskaia, 1970.

Reuven (far left) with his soldier classmates, summer 1970, Kishinev.

Fania and Reuven's wedding, 1973.

Fania and Reuven aboard the *Castalia*, leaving Israel for Paris, summer 1975.

Celebrating Alan's acceptance to UTS, 1994.

Karine with the mayor of the city of Vaughan, receiving the Order of Vaughan award, 2021.

Acknowledgments

I would like to thank my father for giving in and letting me start this book, and I would like to thank Robert Chodos for helping me finish this book - his assistance in editing the final manuscript and proposal was invaluable. A special thanks also goes to my mother for permitting me to steal much of my father's time over the last few years, and an equally special thanks to my late brother, Alan, for being with me in spirit as I undertook the (often painful) journey of this project.

Index